The Rise Framework

THE
RISE
FRAMEWORK

A PROVEN WAY TO INSPIRE, UNIFY, AND ELEVATE YOUR BUSINESS

DOUGLAS HARRISON

FOREWORD BY VICTORIA SASSINE

NEW YORK

LONDON • NASHVILLE • MELBOURNE • VANCOUVER

THE RISE FRAMEWORK

A PROVEN WAY TO INSPIRE, UNIFY, AND ELEVATE YOUR BUSINESS

Published in New York, New York, by Morgan James Publishing. Morgan James is a trademark of Morgan James, LLC. www.MorganJamesPublishing.com

Proudly distributed by Ingram Publisher Services.

Morgan James BOGO™

A **FREE** ebook edition is available for you or a friend with the purchase of this print book.

CLEARLY SIGN YOUR NAME ABOVE

Instructions to claim your free ebook edition:
1. Visit MorganJamesBOGO.com
2. Sign your name CLEARLY in the space above
3. Complete the form and submit a photo of this entire page
4. You or your friend can download the ebook to your preferred device

ISBN 9781631959516 paperback
ISBN 9781631959523 ebook
Library of Congress Control Number: 2022936384

Cover and Interior Design by:
Chris Treccani
www.3dogcreative.net

Morgan James is a proud partner of Habitat for Humanity Peninsula and Greater Williamsburg. Partners in building since 2006.

Get involved today! Visit: www.morgan-james-publishing.com/giving-back

For Adam and Anna.
May your lives be filled with happiness and beauty.

TABLE OF CONTENTS

FOREWORD

It has been an honor to have the privilege of participating in the development of this material and this book. Thank you, Doug, for allowing me to be part of the RISE creation. Your generosity of spirit and knowledge truly illuminates our road.

Thank you, Les Charm and Mike Fetters, for believing in me.

Finally, to my 10,000-plus entrepreneurs from the *Goldman Sachs* program and beyond: I'm awed and humbled to see your toil and joy as you impact your employees, families, and communities. You have let me join in your journey, and I am always in wonder.

This concept—The Rise Framework—and the insights Doug has set forth in this book are game changers in life and industry. His expertise and wisdom in this field are exceptional, and I am so thrilled to see this material published and made accessible to even more entrepreneurs and their networks.

Victoria Sassine

PREFACE

"This is big! I never realized I was playing on everyone else's field when what I have is so uniquely amazing."

This was the illuminating awareness expressed by the CEO of a large municipal bond company when we showed him what his company could really claim and own among its audience compared to what it had been emphasizing. It's a moment I will never forget because it encapsulates the truth of how I serve the people and companies I engage with. The reality is that most people and businesses, with their busy schedules, slip into a mode of saying and doing what they think they are supposed to say rather than declaring why and how they distinctly matter in the world. They lose depth of connection to the people they are intending to attract and end up looking and sounding and feeling like every other company in their industry.

When a company loses clarity of its distinct purpose, it has fallen into what I have come to affectionately refer to as my 10 Mind Traps. These "traps" are mindsets that people adopt when presenting themselves and their offerings to the world that can seriously impair conversion and culture and make everything harder than it needs to be.

The Mind Traps do not apply only to a few. Every single business and person I have ever worked with, including myself, is prone to at least one and typically several of the Mind Traps, depending on the circumstances. Failure to address your Mind Trap at a personal and company level means that every single initiative has a substantial eroding factor working against the outcome. Below is a list of the 10 Mind Traps and how their limitations may play out in a business environment:

1. The **Copy Catter** will continue to present their case in a way that is like their competitors, blending in a non-discriminating way.

2. An **Over Explainer** will overcommunicate what they have to say and will lose customers who get lost in the details and anecdotes.

3. The **Pillar Pitcher** will have key benefits they consistently cite, but may use generic marketing speak to convey them or overlook risk elements in the sales journey, eroding conversion.

4. The **Feature Lister** will continue presenting lengthy feature lists that fail to inspire a vision of how the life of their target will be improved.

5. The **Day Jobber** will keep doing what they do each day, leaving themselves susceptible to changes in the competitive landscape while also overlooking ways to grow their business.

6. The **Tactician** will always be chasing the next tactic with the hope that this will be the one to change their business.

7. The **Defender** will keep defending their choices and miss opportunities to improve or connect.

8. The **Glorifier** will continue to overstate their case to a skeptical buyer, who finds the overuse of adjectives to be an indication that the Glorifier is lying to them.

9. The **Interrogator** will continue to turn off prospects who do not appreciate being asked too many questions to start their engagement without earned reciprocity.

10. The **Schmoozer** will keep losing sales to those prospects who view the wine-and-dine sales approach as an infringement of their personal time or an attempted manipulation of their best self-interests.

Slipping into any of these Mind Traps can leave you feeling frustrated that you cannot sufficiently convey the best and depth of your offering, even though you know it's there. This lack of fully articulated clarity impacts everything. It can feel like you know there is another level up for your sales and marketing, or a way to better inspire and unify your culture, or a smarter way to organize the tactics you pursue . . . but you just don't know how to pull it all together in a neat, powerful package.

You are not alone: almost everyone I have encountered in my life gets tripped up attempting to describe why they distinctly matter because they are too close to their business. The great thing is when you have that clarity, it liberates you and those around you with renewed purpose and inspiration conveyed in a single, complete construct that drives not only sales and marketing, but also unifies operations and human resources around purpose and practices. It works for companies and individuals who are seeking to distinguish themselves.

My name is Doug Harrison. I would like you to know who I am because, for me, business is personal and intensely human. My secret sauce has always been the ability to deeply empathize with the audience you are seeking to attract while recognizing how to package the best of who you are and intend to be in deeply meaningful ways to win more business and relationships. I have seen the impact of good strategy and strong execution on my own life and on the lives of the people I have been privileged to support.

Through our work with hundreds of businesses over the years, my team and I have developed and perfected the Rise Framework—the clarifying, foundational structure every business needs to escape the inefficiencies and disappointments of these Mind Traps and instead elevate their success beyond what they previously thought possible. The 10 Mind Traps are powerful and have never before been recognized. Knowing what to do about them transforms lives and is the most gratifying thing I am privileged to do in this world. Throughout this book, you'll read many personal stories but for now, I want to give you some background on what led me to my solution in the first place.

After graduating from Cornell in the late eighties, I started my first job at Yankelovich Clancy Shulman, a boutique market research and consulting company in Westport, Connecticut. I spent my early years mostly predicting the market potential for new offerings and I had the privilege of learning from Lisa Carter, a tremendous mentor and one of the best in the world at this type of work. Over the course of my life, I have forecasted the business potential for over 500 products, accurately predicting actual sales within 15 percent in 85 percent of cases.

More importantly, we helped optimize those go-to-market propositions, covering messaging, pricing, product configuration, targeting, distribution, etc. It was a great training ground because I learned how adjustments to the product/marketing/messaging mix would impact sales in realistic ways. I eventually was running the strategy division at Yankelovich, and, after a decade, I went out on my own, and the Harrison Group was created.

One of our first projects was completing the global brand architecture for Coca-Cola with my friend and client, Shari Neumann. At the time, Coca-Cola was very focused on authenticity and being "the real thing," which we came to learn was fully established for the brand without any real room for further development. What was underdeveloped was what we referred to as "emotional refreshment," or the opportunity to be uplifted during the consumption occasion. That work became the Happiness campaign for Coca-Cola, and the brand has not stopped its focus on emotional refreshment ever since.

Have you ever used a Coca-Cola Freestyle machine? Those shiny, red, touch-free drink dispensers that allow you to choose from different Coca-Cola drink products to make your own creations? Well, if you have, you're welcome! That was us! Years later, we were Vendor of the Year at Coca-Cola and they remained our top client throughout the entire time I owned the company. Since then, we have worked on nearly every, if not every, single brand in their portfolio in a variety of ways.

My dear friend and mentor, Dr. James Taylor, joined our company, and we built a wealth practice from scratch in partnership with Cara David and our friends at American Express Publishing, where we supported about 50 luxury brands each year with how to sell to people of means more effectively. Paul Lundquist was another partner in our firm who made us the preeminent resource for helping video gaming companies bring new offerings to market, and we were the guys supporting Microsoft around their anti-piracy efforts that made them billions of dollars.

I have also had the good fortune to work on business building and branding and messaging for companies including Under Armour, T-Mobile, The Ritz-Carlton, Amazon, Cayman Islands, American Express, Starbucks, and many others. In addition, I have worked with a number of nonprofits, schools, start-ups, mid-market companies, etc. What I love to do most is inspire people and businesses to discern and cultivate their unique voice for their greatest personal and professional fulfillment. Our process of helping people and companies become the best version of themselves as brands and companies is the same regardless of size.

(If you are interested in knowing more about me as a person, I included a chapter toward the end of the book with more of my life story.)

Social media is filled with influencers who like to give rah-rah speeches that the secret to success is walking your truth, keeping your shoulder to the wheel, or some other superficial maxim. There is a role for individuals like that, but I find their oversimplification of what it takes to be successful both irritating and irresponsible. Getting in the habit of making your bed every morning or knowing that Dr. Seuss was rejected 27 times before getting published is all well and good, but tenacity is barely the beginning.

It's so much easier to talk about these surface tips, but I prefer depth. I want whatever I share with you to mean something and to actually help. I recently encountered a company that has developed a technology to turn cellulose-based waste products going to landfills into a product that is as good as plywood. They have had the tenacity to put 12 years of their lives into this product, but when they go into OverExplainer mode in describing their offering, it makes it nearly impossible to buy from them, which in turn makes them Tacticians as they chase the next hopeful opportunity. Tenacity is not their obstacle. Clarity in their business case, with a business model to support, it will change their lives.

Writing this book and having you read it helps me to fulfill my purpose in this lifetime. I sincerely welcome you to this life-changing approach for how you bring yourself and your offerings to the world.

Doug Harrison

INTRODUCTION

He couldn't see it, but it was there, quietly but unmistakably sabotaging his success.

Richard had come to see me for advice about a problem he had with his steel fabrication company. He had inherited the company from his father, then worked hard to expand it. Sales had plateaued and started to slip.

He walked into my office talking. I saw the AirPods and realized he was in another meeting. After he sat down, he gave me an apologetic index finger, took the last gulp of a Red Bull, crushed the can in his hands, and then looked for a trash can. When his call ended, Richard explained he was sure his problem was not being recognized by more construction companies as a minority-owned business and he wanted me to help him figure out how to make that happen. He was convinced that if he could just solve this one thing, his sales would take off again and he would be back on track. But as we talked about his company, I heard it again—his Mind Trap.

He was caught in the Tactician Mind Trap, chasing his next hope that this would be the action that would open things up again. More than one year earlier, he had spent one million dollars on a fabrication machine that was going to be the catalyst to growth, and six months earlier he had hired a promising new salesperson he felt was the "golden ticket." Now the fabrication machine sat idle more than half the time and the salesperson's golden touch hadn't materialized. These disappointments were now largely forgotten in favor of the next tactic (hope) of a new salvation.

These prior efforts were not the answer because they were all one-off attempts that were not solving the bigger underlying issue. Richard's hidden Mind Trap was distracting him with false hopes that newer and more innovative tactics would transform his company. I'm happy to report that six months later—after our work together—Richard had not only decreased his need for constant caffeine, but his company's sales had increased by 30 percent. And, most importantly, he had a clear vision for the future that he would continue to build on.

After working with over a thousand professionals and businesses, I came to recognize a set of 10 Mind Traps to which people and companies are completely oblivious. These factors are serious obstructions to successfully growing personal brands and businesses, and my clients are consistently unaware of them. I began writing them down and found that the fundamental ways individuals and teams present themselves and their offerings can unwittingly subvert the opportunity to own a more powerful, meaningful, and profitable place in the world.

While there are countless books on ways to improve business, most assume the business can see its issues and simply needs to know how to solve them. Or they oversimplify business success into an expression of their commitment to moving forward. My experience has been that business leadership generally recognizes about half of what it needs to solve; however, roughly half the things that could move them forward more dramatically are not in their lens. Illuminating and understanding these Mind Traps are important steps toward significant personal and professional gains.

Every single company and person we have ever worked with, including myself, slips into at least one, and typically more than one, Mind Trap. None of the Mind Traps are better or worse than the others. They all have some beneficial qualities, but they also work against your best interests to sell more and be more meaningful.

THE 10 MIND TRAPS:

Copy Catter

OverExplainer

Pillar Pitcher

Defender

Tactician

Day Jobber

Feature Lister

Interrogator

Glorifier

Schmoozer

Addressing the Mind Traps is key to greater customer connection, increased sales, and successful growth. I call them Mind Traps to show that these factors are the cause of many hidden problems, rather than personal deficiencies or the next craze in business literature. These are personal to you, your team, and/or your business—and will go on forever, detracting from your success, unless they are somehow interrupted and replaced with a better framework.

Mind Traps are ways of approaching ourselves and our offerings that feel like the right thing to do in the absence of information that would suggest otherwise. My experience has been that once recognition occurs and the individual sees that they are in one of these 10 modes, they immediately recognize how it works against their goals, and they want to shift out of it.

I am also helping clients recognize the Mind Traps in others and use their understanding of them to help the group collectively move forward. This is one of the things I particularly love about this framework. The Traps are recognizable, and consciousness is the first step to being able to make a change.

Make no mistake. When you are caught in one of the 10 Mind Traps, you are working against your own best interest. And all of these are masks that make it hard for those around you to understand why you distinctly matter in the world. Increasingly, that clarity is required by those you seek to serve and connect with. Perhaps more importantly, they are also keeping you away from your feeling of purpose that saps your passion and can leave you performing a series of duties at a time when people want to be engaging with their own life force.

I find a helpful way to visualize how the Mind Traps work against you is to consider three segments. These could be customer segments or prospective employees or partners. One segment is going to convert for sure. They already believe in you or your proposition. Another segment will never convert. Maybe they do not have the money, are loyal to another option or simply do not have the resources. That leaves everyone else in the middle. If your Mind Traps kick in at a level above your competitors, those prospects in the middle are lost, pure and simple.

When I witness this playing out, I see it as analogous to a football team that was training and practicing so hard, only to fumble the ball near the goal line. When putting your proposition out into the world, you are exerting a ton of energy to build the offering, market it, sell it, and support it. To lose a significant number of prospects near the goal line because these Mind Traps present themselves is a major disservice to all the good work you do.

Spend some time to get super clear on recent prospects you have lost, and I can guarantee you that if they entered as part of that middle segment, they are being lost because of Mind Traps. Do this work for your own benefit in the spirit of not wasting any of the precious resources you have committed to getting your prospects near the goal line.

Conversion Funnel
Three Segments

Identifying the problem becomes a catalyst to inspire evolution, and this book lays out the steps to go from Trapped to Illuminated. It involves not only greater empathy for those you serve, but also crafting an entire framework that will evolve sales, marketing, targeting, and operations while unifying the culture of a company founded on a deeper, more meaningful proposition, built around a guiding north star called your Brand Promise.

And this is the perfect time to be introspective and make changes because the world is demanding it. With increased transparency and epidemic-level loneliness, customers are increasingly fed up with traditional sales, branding, and business approaches. People are seeking more meaning and connection with the brands and people they buy from, and they are sick and tired of the generic marketing speak they encounter everywhere.

You cannot say *quality* or *great customer service* anymore. Even the idea of being an *authentic brand* is now overdone and makes people roll their eyes. These statements are now meaningless and get lost in a plethora of other vapid and overused marketing terms. So, without truly understanding your foundational Mind Traps, you and your business will be at the mercy of the ever-changing and more-impatient-than-ever customer base.

In response, individuals and businesses need to have their Mind Traps under control and have all facets of their offerings working together logically. The wonderful, simple aspect of the Mind Traps is that many of the same actions address them all. If the Mind Traps are the method to triage your core brand and business maladies, the Rise Framework is the remedy.

After a 30-plus year career of developing an intuitive understanding of the heart, mind, soul, and wallet of the customer, I have found that empathy is a critical precursor to the success we've experienced. Understanding this first allowed me to combat the Mind Traps, build a Rise Framework, and evolve the success of any person or business. In fact, all 10 Mind Traps occur when businesses and people slip into a lack of empathy while being busy with their daily duties.

While empathy in business is not a new concept, it gains greater strength when combined with the understanding of the 10 Mind Traps and a Rise Framework that will make you stand out now and forever. These foundational concepts go far beyond what we already know about empathy. Empathy goes from becoming a nebulous buzzword to an actionable, driving force.

When you are clear and inspirational in your purpose with a structure that unifies the entire organization together around a distinctive vision, you have something quite wonderful. It touches and improves every process and strategy you implement along the way. **The Rise Framework is a single construct that incorporates sales, marketing, operations, and culture using empathy as a catalyst.**

Most of my working life has been spent doing engagements for big companies, and I have seen their undeniable success after implementing these principles. In recent years, I have spent more of my time with small and mid-market companies. Since these companies are able to implement changes and permeate ideas throughout the company at greater speed, the impact of the Mind Traps and Rise Framework is wonderfully gratifying.

The case studies in this book are real and were completed with small to midsize companies, even though the Rise Framework applies to businesses of any size. I chose these size companies as examples to be more relatable. I am also increasingly finding applications of the Mind Traps for personal branding because of how easily they track with personality.

Nothing thrills me more than helping people break through their own growth ceiling. I have packed this book with all the things I consistently tell people that generate the "Wow, it is so important to know this!" responses. I have put everything in this book you need to take the same path to success my clients have taken. You will have everything necessary to help you illuminate the Mind Traps and develop your own Rise Framework.

The tools presented here will help you focus your efforts, change your perspective, and better inspire your employees and customers. You will be delighted as you simplify a pathway forward. It is truly a pleasure to share this information with you and it is my hope that it will change your life.

PART ONE

ILLUMINATE

Seeing behind Your Own Curtain

Sometimes we feel the effects of a problem without knowing the cause of the problem. In business, it is easy to get lost in fixing small, visible issues. You may feel like you're giving it everything you have, but, somehow, you are feeling like there is something missing. In my personal experience as an entrepreneur, and with the thousand-plus clients I have helped throughout my career, I have learned that the only way out of this exhausting cycle is to identify and deal with the root of your challenges.

There are three consistent underlying causes to business disappointment: not knowing your market, not knowing your business, and not knowing yourself. In this portion of the book, I will take you through the Illuminate phase of our training. We will look at the market forces that affect your customer, introduce you to the 10 Mind Traps, and illustrate how empathy turned to brilliance is the remedy. This insight will set you up perfectly to develop your own Rise Framework, empowering you to assemble all your best and most meaningful assets, find the need in the world you distinctly address, and ultimately create your winning framework.

CHAPTER ONE
THREE LASTING MARKET FORCES

———■———

*"The secret of change is to focus all your energy
not on fighting the old, but on building the new."*
-Socrates

Customers have changed. While I have observed the differences coming on gradually over the last decade, they have quickly and significantly dialed up and settled in during recent years. From what I have seen and studied, there are three fundamental changes in the consumer landscape that are demanding people and businesses evolve their approach to how they bring themselves and their offerings to the world. They are:

- The loneliness epidemic
- The rejection of generic marketing-speak
- The expectation of quality

This evolution in market forces is here to stay. Understanding them will be a competitive advantage for future success.

The Loneliness Epidemic

When my friend Tom finally forced himself to the grocery store last October, he took a deep breath, donned a face mask, and stepped into the surprisingly populated store. He was there for only one item, an item that could not wait for his usual grocery delivery on Saturday: cat food. Recently widowed and still not accustomed to taking care of tabby cat Oliver's daily needs, he had forgotten how low the cat food inventory had become. Now he was out, which had necessitated this trip from his home.

After finding the food, he walked down the aisle to check out. Along the way, an endcap caught his eye. He surprised himself when he grabbed another item and continued toward the checkout. He placed the items on the conveyor belt and, as they made their way to the cashier, she asked to no one in particular, "Did you find everything you were looking for?" Tom responded that he had, and that he had even found something he hadn't come in for. The cashier nodded her head and the cat food was quickly beeped across the scanner and placed into a plastic bag.

Then the cashier picked up the second item, a small box. She paused for a moment and looked up. Tom immediately returned her gaze with just a hint of expectation to talk about his impulse buy. The cashier opened her lips to speak, but decided against it, put her head back down, and put the box into the bag. Tom took the bag, sighed, and walked out with the cat food he needed and the box of birthday candles he wished he needed. On the way to the car, he calculated—his late wife would have been seventy-two.

A study completed by Cigna found that 61 percent of Americans feel lonely.[1] If we conservatively leave out all children and focus on just the adults in this country, that is over 150 million people.[2] That is an awful lot of people out there looking for greater connection as a means to greater fulfillment.

We now live in a reality where our world is working through deeply divisive issues. Nothing seems to work easily anymore, and it can feel really isolating. I don't see this getting solved anytime soon. The majority of Americans are tired of discord and they are emotionally moving on with the pursuit of peace and ease by going inward. I think brands and businesses that help connect and provide places where people can feel like they are part of something good in the world will do well in the years ahead.

Further feeding our loneliness in the world of business and commerce is that nearly all of us have been taught how to operate under a standard of professionalism that keeps us apart. It is so ingrained in culture now that we don't even think about it. Being professional means keeping your distance, not getting personal, not sharing yourself, and not getting too close to why your customer might want something. It now seems even inappropriate to ask a customer about something as benign as a birthday candle. It is everything we don't need during a loneliness epidemic!

Doing something because it has always been done that way is the perfect bedrock for disruptive innovation. When something becomes a normalized practice that is no longer questioned, one of my favorite things to do is to suggest we ask ourselves, "Are we truly happy with this as our standard operating procedure, or is there something better we could do?"

I think we can do better. Much, much better. And in business, it starts with how we talk to our customers. Most businesses and employees operate out of a transactional mindset when we really need to be more relationally focused. What's even more crazy is that I find while most people are seeking greater connection, they are looking for others to take the first step or make the first move.

Fortune favors the brave, and today that means being willing to let the old version of professionalism die. This book will bring up many marketing traditions that need to be buried and done with, but "professionalism" is the first. And, in its place, we can establish a new definition that includes the risk of vulnerability and an openness to greater connection.

The Rejection of Generic Marketing Speak

Take a look at this tagline: "*Where your family comes first.*"

A non-exhaustive Google search shows that this is the slogan used by: Bayada Home Health Care, Best Family Home Care, First Family Insurance, Premier Care Pediatrics, Family First Dental, Family Doctors of Green Valley, Barker Law Firm, Fears Family Funeral Home, Keller Williams Hudson Valley United, and more.

"*Banking Your Way*" is the mantra of Discover Online Banking, Chase, Zions Bank, CUA, Fort Sill National Bank, Scotiabank, and Camden National.

"*Luxury living at affordable prices*" is touted by Orr Street Lofts, The Mezz, West Village Group, Greater Coastal Management, Cobble Creek Apartments, Summit Chase Apartments, and others.

Over the years, I have identified a significant number of trends for businesses, and the one I have been preaching about recently is that people, to put it bluntly, are tired of the BS. They are looking for meaning. For years, standard marketing jargon has worked, and it is amazing it has survived this long. With our exposure to so many brands through social media, consumers have heard enough of the same marketing verbiage. They want something new to take its place. It's almost as if every marketer went to the same school of marketing and was taught to use this limited library of vocabulary when trying to sell something. These words are now so frequently encountered they have become marketing's comfortable suite of turn-to language. Once you become aware of generic marketing speak, it will bug you every time you see it!

The incremental challenge for marketers is that these phrases feel so good when they use them because they seem like they are the polished expressions of the right way to say things. They used to be, but today, these types of expressions under the best of circumstances cause you to blend into a sea of mass monotony. Under the worst of circumstances, these words irritate and anger prospective buyers because the language is viewed as intentionally manipulative.

Consider these additional phrases that are only a small fraction of what consumers are frustrated with in today's marketing speak. Each category in this list has many more that customers expect to hear daily. Honestly, I cannot decide which of these deserves the biggest eye roll . . .

- "Finding greater insights through deeper data interpretation"
- "Transformative solutions to challenging problems"
- "Doing business your way"
- "We are right on the corner and right on the price!"
- "Your trusted resource"
- "Building a better world for our employees, partners, and communities"
- "Providing actionable insights"
- "Your business, our priority"
- "Getting you there in comfort"
- "Delivering quality you can rely on"
- "We listen to your needs"
- "100 percent mom approved"
- "Providing value-added services and solutions"

The list is obviously much longer, but the common quality to most marketing language is that it is just plain not effective. Generic marketing speak is the lazy approach to conveying your proposition, and sellers do not realize it because it is standard practice to use it. Many experienced marketers think this vocabulary helps their sales numbers, but it actually works against them in today's market of informed consumers.

Back when I had my market research and consulting company, everyone in the industry used to say, "We deliver actionable insights." I went to a medical device convention and was walking around the exhibition hall that literally had 1,000 exhibitors on hand. I could not tell what any of them did and there had to be about a dozen that were saying some version of "Finding greater insights through deeper data interpretation."

Seeing it at this scale made me realize how blind most businesses are to overused marketing vocabulary. If you're anything like me, when you see it now, you will want to go up, cross it out, and write something else!

Companies continue to say what they think they are supposed to say instead of what they mean about why they really matter in the world. Most struggle when I ask them to articulate,

"What is the problem that you uniquely solve in the world for those you serve?"

The reason we struggle to answer that question is because we all get so busy with our day-to-day requirements in our own environments that we lose perspective. On top of that, we are trained on how we are "supposed" to talk and convey our offerings, rather than speaking our truth from the depth of our hearts.

I hear marketers who say, "I get inside the head of my customer," and then I watch them still proceed to talk *at* their prospects rather than envision the conclusions those individuals will make using all their senses. This is a big deal!

Avoid operating out of what you think you are supposed to say and start operating from a space of taking responsibility for the conclusions your audience will make about you through everything they can learn, see, hear, sense, or feel.

When you start operating in a mode of taking responsibility for the conclusions your audience will draw about you, rather than simply doing your job, you immediately develop empathy and change your approach!

This practice is so pervasive that I can also easily fall into the generic marketing speak trap. My practice has become to write what I want to convey about the brand, and then make an extra pass to test language, which determines if I have fallen into the use of generic marketing speak. I do this through a process of deep imagining or empathy of how I would feel as a prospect if I were to hear my language. I ask, "How would I feel if I heard this?" Would . . .

- it seem unique?
- I feel inspired?
- it cause me to act?

If I can give myself a "Yes," then I am golden. Otherwise, there is more work to be done!

We have found the marketing language that leads to higher conversion has three common aspects. First, it must be *truthful* and reflect the actual workplace values shared by those who labor within the company. Second, it must be *meaningful* in the hearts and minds of the target. And third, it must be *distinctive* with respect to the competition.

Truthful.

Meaningful.

Distinctive.

These qualities are even more important because in order to be successful in today's market, businesses have to find something more specific than just quality to prove their worth.

The Expectation of Quality

The panicked urgency in Jeff's voice was unmistakable. "What are we going to do?"

Jeff was the CMO for a premier lineup of five-star hotels. Their facilities were exceptional, the staff was attentive, the spa was impeccable, and the packages offered were attractive. But, despite all this attention to quality and detail, the hotel was underperforming.

Exasperated, Jeff pleaded, "How are we supposed to stand out?"

He was experiencing a new market factor: the expectation of quality. Multiple dynamics have been playing out over the last several years that have increasingly elevated customers' expectations of quality performance standards. This evolution started back in the Great Recession of 2008 when buyers scaled back their buying, which meant competition to win customers intensified, and the quality bar to stay in business was raised. Around that same time, customer reviews became prominent and widespread, meaning companies could no longer get away with delivering marginal offerings. Most businesses today are acutely attuned to customer feedback, and many will do just about anything to avoid negative posts on any review or social media website.

Quality is increasingly expected across every category. You don't see cars pitching their powertrain warranty anymore. A car is expected to last 100,000 or more miles with few if any problems. Airbnb, Yelp, Google reviews, Facebook reviews, and Uber driver ratings are now hugely responsible for the success or failure of individual brands or even people.

There are two things that businesses can do about this and ideally, they will do both.

The first is that, when quality becomes expected, businesses have no choice but to elevate their values as an aspect of their value proposition. Values have always been part of a brand proposition, but today they are much more important and much more on display. Values need to be deep and complete and true. For a time, companies could get away with giving a portion of their proceeds to a charity to check the values box. Those days are over.

Today, people are increasingly seeking to find the best of themselves being reflected back at them in the brands that they buy. When I buy Patagonia, I know the owner of that company designed an offering that reflected his best values of the world he wanted to explore. When I buy Toms, I believe they really care about giving shoes to people who need them.

The second strategy is to dig deeper into what makes your offering more exceptional as a product or experience. For sure you cannot simply say you provide a quality product or service. Instead, you must look deeper and develop the proof that you are doing something special.

This can take a little time to figure out how to articulate, since most companies have not fully contemplated how to express the *wonderfulness* of their sausage making. But those wonderful aspects are there, or you wouldn't be in business. It's just a matter of figuring out how to effectively identify it, improve it, claim it, and convey it. The tools I provide will help you to do this wonderfully.

A tile store can't simply have nice-looking tiles. They have to offer visualization tools for you to envision your home with alternative designs, with salespeople who have design sensibilities to elevate your best home life, before you will pay them even a penny. A cosmetic surgery center and medical spa can't just do facelifts and breast augmentations. They have to help dreams become real for those who wish to see themselves in a new way, providing care in a loving environment with a full suite of solutions. These are just a couple initial examples of bringing greater depth to a conventional offering. Case studies in the later chapters illustrate the path to discovering and developing these strategies.

The transactional model most marketers and sellers use dehumanizes the customer whether they like to admit it or not. I run into marketers all the time who have "figured out" the secret sauce by doing A/B testing of their ad campaigns. They brag they have figured out that when they push this campaign out, they can count on an "XX percent" conversion rate. I love that ability, but I don't hear a great deal of love for the customer being expressed. Why do they have the word "relationship" in CRM tools if they are not relational at all? Their dominant use is a mathematical process for determining how many and which sequence of hits in a drip campaign will turn into a prospect or customer. They are not designed particularly well to support engagement along the way or to nurture those disengaged. In reality, they don't really care. They just want customers to buy.

I don't mind that companies operate in a transactional mode. I get it, because companies need to make money and I fully support using digital tools to drive sales. I'm just not convinced long-term that a transactional mindset is sustainable since consumers crave relationships.

It is from this thought process that I began to pay attention to all the specific ways businesses were missing their opportunities to create relationships. These became the 10 Mind Traps. Knowing yours and working to overcome them is the first step in helping

your business provide an offering with greater meaning and cultivate greater connection with your customers.

CONSIDERATIONS...

- Does the idea that **we are living in a world that is lonely and craving greater connection** resonate with you?

- **Check your own language for generic marketing speak** and be on the lookout for it in your travels to help you be mindful of avoiding it in your future communications.

- **How seriously do you take ownership of the conclusions your audience makes about you?** How might you adjust your approach if you get serious about this responsibility?

CHAPTER TWO
THE 10 MIND TRAPS

"Affliction comes to us, not to make us sad but sober;
not to make us sorry but wise."
-H.G. Wells

There are endless good ideas. And there are countless people who work to turn those ideas into businesses. The tricky part is being able to get other people to buy into the idea. Selling is both an individual and an organizational pursuit. Salespeople bring their own personalities to a discussion about an organization's offering. Conversely, the brand identity of an organization can be a strong force in either unifying or derailing the selling efforts of those who work there.

Over the course of my career, every business and salesperson has primary and secondary Mind Traps they slide into that work against their best interests. They exist regardless of how well things are going at the company. Everyone finds upside! Eight of the 10 Mind Traps can emerge either at a company level or at an individual level. The last two only exist at an individual level. While some Mind Traps are professionally driven and some are personality driven, every Mind Trap sabotages success because they seriously detract from the conclusions we would like our prospects and employees to see in what we are offering.

Introduction to the Mind Traps

The Mind Traps are the tendencies individuals unconsciously slip into with their business, sales, and branding. They operate at a personal level and at a business level. I have never met anyone, including myself, who does not have at least one, and usually more than one, Mind Trap. They can be institutional or situational in nature.

None of the Mind Traps are good and all hurt our sales, waste resources, and inhibit our ability to inspire prospects. They are always floating under the surface, just waiting for the right moment to pop up and work against our best interests. Our Mind Traps have enormous opportunity costs because they cause us to waste our time and money on suboptimal approaches when we could be doing so much better. The good news is that they are fixable with the right tools—and this book gives you those tools!

At their core, the Mind Traps should be viewed as catalysts for change. Though I mentioned earlier that they are not good things to hold on to, they do have some positive qualities and can be good when viewed as the first steps to making productive changes. Our Mind Traps are merely a starting point to finding out what type of change we need to make.

So, hello. My name is Doug. I am a recovering Tactician and Day Jobber, and sometimes I am a Feature Lister and Copy Catter. I know we can cure our Mind Traps together!

A company will have its own Mind Traps, which may be the same or different from the Mind Traps of the individuals who work there. When setting out to work on your Mind Traps, you must be intentional about addressing both levels. The Mind Trap presented at a company level will be most influenced by company leadership and those individuals who are responsible for sales and marketing communications. If they are a Copy Catter, then they will present the business much like everyone else in the category. Each employee will also add their own Mind Trap of being a Schmoozer, Glorifier, etc., which adds another layer into the mix that needs to be addressed.

For sellers, this need manifests itself when companies spend time thinking about what they need and want to tell customers about the importance of their offering, following up with how well they provide it. The amount of time contemplating the conclusions a prospect will draw, based on the sum of everything they can learn about the offering, is little and sometimes none. When you shift your mindset and begin taking responsibility for the conclusions that someone draws based on the sum of their experiences, you see things as your customer sees them, which is ultimately what determines conversion. Deep empathy for what your audience most resonates with combined with finding the most meaningful expression of your best qualities are the keys to distinctly mattering to those you seek to serve.

Amount of time spent thinking about what needs to get done and what needs to be said

Amount of time thinking about the conclusions prospects draw based on the totality of their encounters with your offering

For example, in helping my daughter's private school, I challenged them on something as simple as giving a school tour. I said, "You think your job is to show prospects around the school at that point in time. It isn't! Your job is to set up a set of experiences and encounters that will lead them to the conclusion that this school is delivering on its Promise. When you think in those terms, the meaning of the school tour should change dramatically." My daughter's school is one of the case studies, and you'll see what happened when they started taking responsibility for what prospective parents and students thought about them.

I was just looking at a website last night for a friend who is running a diabetes-monitoring company. Their device attaches to the body and impressively measures glucose levels every minute, sending alarms when there are meaningful changes. This company has spent a lot of time focused on what its device does and how easy it is to change the patch every 14 days.

My first thought from the patient perspective was that this could be a total nightmare. *Am I going to get an alarm every time I wait one hour too long to eat, or I decide to cheat a little with something outside my regular diet? And then what happens? Is my doctor going to get a note that I was naughty again?* This is a perfect example of a company that is so focused on what they do, they miss why they matter. While one benefit is that you no longer have to prick yourself, the company does not have a deeper understanding of how the device actually supports the best lives of its users. They provide no before and after picture of how life is improved with this device relative to alternatives. I see this kind of approach all the time and it is always driven by the need to "tell you what I do" rather than "why I matter."

Professional vs. Personality

It also turns out that the Mind Traps can be considered in two categories. Some Mind Traps are more personality driven while others are more professionally driven.

Professionally Driven

- Copy Catter
- Pillar Pitcher
- Tactician
- Feature Lister
- Glorifier

Personality Driven

- OverExplainer
- Defender
- Day Jobber
- Interrogator
- Schmoozer

For those with personality driven Mind Traps, you have probably been operating for the better part of a lifetime, so changes will require a great deal of practice. But it can be done!

Professionally driven Mind Traps have been learned on the job, so they tend to be less difficult to shift. A change in corporate branding can be surprisingly beneficial at remediating professionally driven Mind Traps.

A quick snapshot of each Mind Trap is offered below. There are more detailed profiles with case studies for each Mind Trap later in the book so you can see how it is possible to overcome them.

The Copy Catter

Most often, being in **Copy Catter** mode means intentionally examining one's competitors to see how they are presenting themselves to the world. When they find consistency in the way their competitors present themselves, they conclude this must be the way the job is done and they create a very similar framework. They are merely following the way they are "supposed" to present themself to prospective customers/clients.

It results in companies saying what they think they are supposed to say instead of *what* they really mean and *why* they really matter. The challenge for Copy Catters is that, thanks to overused marketing speak, people are increasingly tired of hearing the same old jargon.

Copy Catters' communications end up being adequate but not distinctive, as all the brands end up blending into a sea of monotony. It may seem obvious when stated out loud, but you have to bring incremental benefits to the table in order to win a disproportionate percentage of prospects. I recently spoke to an architect who summed up his experiences with engineering firms that were pitching him. "They all showed me their portfolio of projects, told me they do quality work, and that they were passionate about doing it. None of them gave me a single distinctive thing that they did, so I just kept using the company I was working with because I know them, and they do solid work. The companies pitching me gave me nothing incremental as to why I should switch to them."

Professional service firms like lawyers, accountants, architects, engineering firms, financial services, medical practices, and even solar companies are almost all Copy Catters.

The Copy Catter in a nutshell:
- Looks at key competitors to determine how to present themselves
- Attempts to incorporate their own distinctions, but still mostly blends in as similar
- Evidence suggests they are like everybody else

Win: Prospects who are having a problem with their current provider

Lose: Prospects who see little that tells them to work with the Copy Catter vs. someone else

The OverExplainer

The **OverExplainer** Mind Trap comes from not having a clear, concise purpose for being. The result is the seller adds more and more content or descriptors that come to their minds during their pitch, with the hope that one of their points will stick. The common sales approach I hear from an OverExplainer is "I keep talking to the prospect until I find the point where their eyes light up, and then I focus there." What I often tell the OverExplainer is that the moment they saw the "light in the eye" of the prospect was when the prospect figured out the excuse they were going to use to get out of the discussion!

The problem with the OverExplainer approach is that buyers want clarity in purpose and expect brands to know what that is. Some buyers are willing to invest some time to see if they can figure out the purpose of your proposition, but most will simply give up, recognizing they have lived most of their lives without your proposition, so chances are they will be fine without it.

OverExplainers are intelligent but often scattered individuals who have lost track of their customer because they are so caught up in what they believe is a list of topics or anecdotes that should be motivating to a purchaser (or just interesting to hear). With all the information the OverExplainer knows so well, how could someone not find a reason to join in or purchase? The reality is the customer gets lost in the confusion usually much earlier in the conversation and is simply looking for a pause to break free.

This Mind Trap is a little more challenging to shift because it is more personality driven than professionally driven. I picture OverExplainers growing up as the kids at the dinner table who were happy telling their parents long stories about what happened in school that day. Passionate entrepreneurs, schools, and philanthropies are common OverExplainer categories.

The OverExplainer in a nutshell:
- Passionate and inspired about what they do
- Communications will meander across several topic areas
- Lots of storytelling and anecdotal experiences

Win: Prospects who are drawn to the OverExplainer's passion

Lose: Prospects who can't figure out the conclusion they should draw or who fear the OverExplainer may be disorganized

The Pillar Pitcher

 Pillar Pitchers think deeply about their value proposition and the core—usually three—Pillars that support it. The challenge is these Pillars are seller centric instead of buyer centric. In other words, the presentation is built around the mindset of, "This is what you need to know about what I have to offer."

More focused than OverExplainers, the telltale sign of the Pillar Pitcher are sellers who have done the work of recognizing three to

four underlying Pillars that support their value proposition. These are the offerings to which my *Three Shiny Apples* parable applies.

Once upon a time, there was a boy who was trying to sell a basket of apples in the market. He put his three shiniest apples on top. A man came to buy apples. The boy immediately showed him his basket, with the three shiny, prominently displayed apples. Then, the boy picked up the three apples and put the rest of the basket behind the counter. He showed the man each shiny apple and talked about how wonderfully crisp and ripe and sweet they were. The man wanted to know more about *all* the apples. But the boy was so intent on showing just the three apples, the man was worried the others were not as nice.

The man became skeptical—he started rummaging around the boy's fruit stand, trying to see the other apples in the basket and on display. He even talked to passersby to see if they had ever purchased apples from the boy. He wanted to make sure that he was buying an entire basket of good apples. But the boy continued to proudly praise the three shiny apples, so the man left, sure that the boy's focus on the three shiny apples meant that he was trying to sell a basket containing many bad apples.

The risk with a Pillar Pitcher is that without an understanding of how the Pillars work within the larger framework, and without the ability to describe how the Pillars connect to the Brand Promise and a customer's best self, a buyer will naturally resolve to find a "bad apple." They will look for any negative details they might discover online, in a social media review, in a showroom, from other points you made, in things you don't say, on packaging, from friends, etc. Even if the Pillars are solid, customers will reject the entire proposition with the belief they are likely being lied to.

Buyers are inherently looking to avoid risk. The reward when they find a blemish in the basket of apples that justifies a rejection is that they get to keep their money and feel like a smart shopper. Sellers sell thinking everyone *wants to buy* products. The reality is prospects are looking for reasons *not* to buy.

The Pillar Pitcher in a nutshell:
- Will rely on two to three "shiny apples" (the Pillars) to pitch their offering
- Tends to pitch Pillars that may not be adequately distinctive, can fall into generic marketing speak, or may not have adequate evidence to support them
- Overlooks risk elements they failed to address (buyers buy the basket of apples and are looking for a bad apple)

Win: Prospects who like the clarity of the proposition
Lose: Prospects who recognize risk elements or who find the Pillars to be generic

The Feature Lister

Feature Listers are often in businesses with offerings that contain many distinctive, measurable traits and there is a heavy focus on product specifications in the development process. Sellers naturally want to show the magnitude of their product by presenting a lengthy feature list. But the greater vision of how the product changes the customer's life (the before and after picture of the core problem being solved) gets lost. With that loss goes the opportunity to create the emotional impact that is the ultimate motivation for purchase.

Many salespeople love to be Feature Listers because it is easy. Their mindset is, *If I can convince a customer to hear my pitch (which is the product features) and if they don't buy, it is the product's fault—or, if not the product, the price point.* Ultimately Feature Listers do not see how their inability to convey a vision of a product's positive impact on the life of their prospect limits their ability to sell. Feature Listers are very common in technology, medical device, and biotech companies.

This is also the dominant mindset in private aviation, which was just fascinating for me to witness. I thought the sale of private aircraft would be filled with emotion, but time after time, I would witness salespeople turn their jets into lists of features around capacity, speed, fuel economy, headroom, controls, etc. What inevitably would happen was that each competitor would have a feature(s) the others didn't, so the buyer would use those feature gaps as leverage to lower the price of aircraft as much as possible. Being a Feature Lister, amazingly enough, does not elevate your proposition, but can actually commoditize it.

The Feature Lister in a nutshell:
- Presents lengthy feature lists attempting to win prospects by overwhelming them with evidence of their benefits
- Fails to inspire a vision of how the prospect's life will be improved . . . painting the before and after picture
- Creates risks that features may not all be delivered or can coexist effectively

Win: Prospects who tend to be more technical and fact focused.
Lose: Prospects who feel overwhelmed or who are looking for more emotional inspiration.

The Day Jobber

The **Day Jobber** is busy doing today what they did the day before, which will be the same thing that they will do tomorrow. One day blends into the next in a list of daily tasks that need to get done. These businesses may be stable and comfortable for years, doing about the same revenue year over year, but are vulnerable to escalating costs or disruptive solutions.

These entities are most present in long-standing and local businesses. They don't require much in the way of sales and marketing because there is a steady established base of customers. Often, Day Jobbers don't like selling very much. Instead, they like doing their trade and have found that if they do a good job, they will get repeat business and most likely some referrals to keep the business going.

The risk is when an industry disruptor like Airbnb or Uber comes along to destroy the life the Day Jobber knew and loved. Or it may be the dry cleaner that is doing great until a new cleaner company opens with faster service or home delivery. If a Day Jobber is only interested in maintaining the status quo, they may not survive long term.

The Day Jobber in a nutshell:

- Will do today what they did yesterday, which will be what they will do again tomorrow
- Likes doing what they do more than selling what they do
- Is often unclear or uncomfortable stating their value proposition when asked

Win: Prospects who are drawn to the reliability of the Day Jobber and their offering

Lose: Prospects who never become aware of their offering or who receive a weak pitch when requested

The Tactician

The Tactician is one of the more common Mind Traps. Businesses inherently need new initiatives to grow and build. The Tactician emerges when a company looks for new ways to grow and make more money. They go through a review of different *ways* they might be able to make more money: they could hire a new salesperson, buy a new piece of equipment, target a new audience, run a new promotion, or line-extend an existing offering, for example. All are considered in the context of "I think that might help me grow and make more money."

Ultimately, the company settles on a tactic and pulls the trigger. The Tactician is confusing a tactic for a strategy. The tactics end up being short-term in nature, disjointed, and mixed with respect to their degree of success. Whatever idea is pursued will potentially be supplanted by the next idea, which is usually necessary because the prior idea did not materialize to the desired result.

The struggle continues because the Tactician's quest is to continually come up with the next idea to grow or make money, always assuming the new idea will be better than the last one. The craziest part for a Tactician is that previous tactics that once held all this hope just sort of fade away and are forgotten, about to be replaced with the next tactic . . . hence the image of the human on the hamster wheel. The opportunity for the Tactician is to have a stronger, more powerful understanding of why they matter in the world and how they are going to get there. When they have a well-defined strategy, chosen tactics hold a continuity in purpose that gets them out of chasing a series of one-off ideas.

The Tactician in a nutshell:

- Chases the next tactic, hoping this will be the one to take off
- Tactics are one-offs and often are not fully baked before launching
- Forgets the previous tactic as the new shiny opportunity surfaces

Win: Prospects who are drawn to the tactic

Lose: Prospects because the tactic is not fully integrated into a deeper purpose for the business and lack of commitment comes through to prospects

The Defender

The Defender feels a great deal of pressure to have all of the answers figured out and have the need to prove to others they are consistently right. Defenders often convince themselves they are good listeners, when in fact their time in discussions is spent explaining why they made their respective decisions or why all your good suggestions are things they have already thought of, but just have not done yet because of limited time or money. Defenders can be tremendously successful if they are right but are huge failures if they are wrong. The challenge is many will never know which camp they are in.

Another great signal of a Defender is when someone laments their customers "don't get it," how if they only understood why they needed this or that, they would want the Defender's product. If you are waiting for your customers to "get it," you are in a whole bunch of trouble, because they don't have to "get" anything. They are living just fine without your product. If you ever find yourself having the urge to say, "They don't get it," tell yourself, "It's my job to find a way for this to work for my target."

People who work for Defenders struggle because their ideas don't have a place to land. I personally will not work with committed Defenders. It tends to be a futile, uphill battle and many Defenders who don't acknowledge this Mind Trap ultimately can lose control of their business.

The Defender in a nutshell:
- Defends their choices and misses opportunities to improve
- May blame the customer for "not getting it"
- Errs too far in the direction of defending choices and staying in the problem versus improving and being in the solution

Win: Prospects who are drawn to the Defender's conviction
Lose: Prospects, and potentially employees, who feel the Defender values his or her needs over theirs

The Glorifier

The Glorifier has decided that the grander the adjectives they can surround their nouns with, the more buyers will be convinced of the merits of the Glorifier's mission, ideas, or product. Their hope is that their lofty words will lift the appeal of their proposition. Glorifiers can also be inward facing where they place a higher priority on feeling good about themselves (we are all amazing people here doing amazing things) which comes at the expense of delivering the best offering they can through a more self-critical lens. Inward-facing Glorifiers are less comfortable with what they view as self-criticism and their offerings can have weaknesses overlooked as a result.

Inward-facing Glorifiers can be present anywhere. Outward-facing Glorifiers are more present in luxury brands and we have worked with several of them over the years. In our partnership with American Express, we monitored and studied the hearts and spending of wealthy and affluent individuals. One of the things we observed was that most of the individuals doing the creative communications work for luxury brands were not affluent themselves. The result was they imagined what it meant and felt like to be a person of means, based on what they had seen portrayed on television.

This assumed the stereotype of people who were a bit arrogant with a sense of superiority to everyone else. The reality is that the vast majority of individuals who attained wealth did so in their lifetime and came from middle- and lower-class upbringings. Most of them did not relate to all of the hype marketers want to throw at them. I have grown to have a real distaste for the term "badge value," which lots of marketers casually throw around associated with wealthy people showing off their luxury items. There is some truth to badge value, but my experience is that people first buy products based on what it communicates to how they want to feel about themselves.

If you are interested in learning more about selling to affluent and wealthy individuals, I would encourage you to read my other two books written with Dr. James Taylor, titled *The New Elite* and *Selling to the New Elite*. They both provide clear examples on how to sell in the affluent marketing landscape.

The Glorifier in a nutshell:
- Overstates their case through the overuse of grand adjectives or self-importance
- May cause buyers to feel the Glorifier is lying to them
- Creates an "after picture" that is misaligned with how the buyer feels about their life

Win: Prospects who are drawn to the vision being created
Lose: Prospects who feel they are being oversold and deceived

The Interrogator

 The Interrogator exists exclusively as a personal Mind Trap and not as a company Mind Trap. Interrogators believe they can outmaneuver prospects by dominating the early sales pitch with an excessive amount of questions they have not yet earned the right to ask. In their minds, the best way to win the deal is by asking the prospect a lot of questions with the intent of identifying the best means to speak their language and hit on the primary points they believe the prospect will want to hear.

Interrogators convince themselves this is the best way to approach selling, because they equate asking questions with being customer centric. They do this because they are less comfortable or lack confidence in their ability to convey a concise elevator pitch that invites questions and conversation.

The challenge is that buyers believe every piece of information they give to an Interrogator will be used in a clumsy and obviously manipulative way to get them to purchase. Interrogators are very liberal in the number of questions they feel entitled to ask, and if the prospect answers some of the questions, they take it as a signal to just keep going. Oftentimes the seller is not even sure where his or her questions are intended to take the sales lead!

The opportunity for Interrogators is to recognize the need to earn the right to ask questions through a process of escalating reciprocity where they need to go first in creating moments of vulnerability. This, in turn, will inspire a willingness in the prospect to share more about themselves and what they are looking for. Interrogators are most present in commission sales categories.

The Interrogator in a nutshell:

- Asks too many questions too early in their pitch
- Values questions over a clear and consistent value proposition
- Mistakes questioning for being client centric

Win: Prospects who accept being fully questioned early in the sales process

Lose: Prospects who are irritated by presumptive questioning

The Schmoozer

The Schmoozer is also a personal Mind Trap, not present at a company level. Schmoozers rely on their ability to be likable or to create situations where the prospect can take a break from the daily grind with cocktails, dinner, a trip, some golf, etc. They rely on relationships to sell and, for those who are good at it, this can work very well. However, many Schmoozers are heavily committed to this tactic at the expense of all others. It can become the only way they feel comfortable selling.

Some Schmoozers can be overly dependent on other people in their company to do things for them. They may require considerable help in the areas of proposal writing, technical support, or company leadership to finish closing the sale for them. In their mind, getting the appointment set is their job, assuring themselves (and others) that it took a great deal of finesse and relationship building to make it happen. They feel that others who do not possess their skill can help finish getting the deal over the line or writing the content that will support the emails, marketing materials, proposals, etc.

Being a Schmoozer only becomes problematic if a person overly relies on relationships at the expense of product and branding. Why? Because not all prospects want to be wooed by a Schmoozer. A Schmoozer might get past the gatekeeper only to get shut down by the ultimate decision maker, who may view schmoozing as detracting from substance in the product offering or an outright attempt to manipulate their purchasing. It is important to be able to adapt to the personality traits with which your prospect wants to engage. Schmoozers are present in higher ticket categories where entertaining clients is an accepted practice and commission sales are common.

The Schmoozer in a nutshell:
- Has a large network that blends business and social engagement
- Can value network and connections over conversions and margin
- May require incremental technical or prospecting support

Win: Prospects who like more socially oriented selling

Lose: Prospects who don't want to be sold socially. Organization may not be designed to support the Schmoozer

Why Knowing Your Mind Trap Matters

In summary, failure to address your Mind Trap at a personal and company level means that every single initiative has a substantial eroding factor working against the outcome. This is how the limiting Mind Trap continues to play out, no matter what other things the entity may attempt to pursue:

1. The **Copy Catter** will continue to present their case in a way that is like their competitors, blending in a non-discriminating way.
2. An **OverExplainer** will overcommunicate what they have to say and will lose customers who get lost in the details and anecdotes.
3. The **Pillar Pitcher** will have key benefits they consistently cite, but may use generic marketing speak to convey them or overlook risk elements in the sales journey, eroding conversion.
4. The **Feature Lister** will continue presenting lengthy feature lists that fail to inspire a vision of how the life of their target will be improved.
5. The **Day Jobber** will keep doing what they do each day, leaving themselves susceptible to changes in the competitive landscape while also overlooking ways to grow their business.
6. The **Tactician** will always be chasing the next tactic with the hope that this will be the one to change their business.
7. The **Defender** will keep defending their choices and miss opportunities to improve or connect.
8. The **Glorifier** will continue to overstate their case to a skeptical buyer, who finds the overuse of adjectives to be an indication that the Glorifier is lying to them.
9. The **Interrogator** will continue to turn off prospects who do not appreciate being asked too many questions to start their engagement without earned reciprocity.
10. The **Schmoozer** will keep losing sales to those prospects who view the wine-and-dine sales approach as an infringement of their personal time or an attempted manipulation of their best self-interests.

And so it goes until the Mind Traps are illuminated and addressed. Companies and individuals will be unable to optimize all the big and small details of how they bring themselves and their propositions to the world until they face them. This is an important first step in making your sales and branding dreams come true! The Mind Traps are the starting point to building the Rise Framework, which we are going into in Chapter Four.

I encourage you to pick the one or two Mind Traps that most resonate with you as the ones that are working against your best interests. Consider the Mind Traps from two vantage points.

The first will be your company's lens, which may suffer from a Mind Trap(s) that is driven by the persons who are responsible for sales and marketing. Second, everyone on the team will have their own Mind Traps to be addressed separately.

You may also consider the Mind Traps from a personal brand vantage point. As you seek to attract the positions you desire, be aware of how you are presenting yourself in the context of what you want your various audiences to conclude about you. Remember, you are responsible for the conclusions others make about you.

There is a good chance you will also recognize secondary Mind Traps you and your company might feel a need to address. Don't get too distracted with too many. The secondary Mind Traps will also get attended to by addressing the primary Mind Traps. The greatest thing about our Rise Framework is that regardless of whatever Mind Trap(s) you may experience, the steps to overcoming them share many common elements. And it all begins with the deepest of empathy for those you seek to serve.

CONSIDERATIONS...

- **Which of the Mind Traps do you most resonate with** either at a personal or company level?
- **Keep in mind that you may gravitate toward different Mind Traps under different circumstances.** You can always use them as a filter to consider if you are bringing your best self forward in any environment.
- This is the first time you will consider how your Mind Traps can work against your goals. **Start recognizing more specifically the situations where your Mind Traps(s) has worked against you.** What might you start shifting?

CHAPTER THREE

THE POWER OF INTENSE, ROLE-REVERSING EMPATHY

———————— ▬ ————————

"You never really understand a person until you consider things from his point of view—until you climb into his skin and walk around in it."
-Atticus Finch in *To Kill A Mockingbird*, Harper Lee

In many ways, life is an extremely individual experience, but life becomes richer when we operate in the spirit of true service and consideration to those we seek to inspire. It is human nature to operate and interact with others with our own perspective and needs at the forefront. But now, more than ever, there is an immense need to shift from *first-person* to *third-person* thinking—especially in business.

Businesses almost always operate out of a mode of "here is what we do and how we do it" instead of thinking about what and how they need to present themselves in the world to drive a set of conclusions they seek to inspire in the minds of their target. This is first-person thinking: telling people what they should know about you.

Third-person thinking, on the other hand, means getting inside your customers' hearts and minds to imagine how they might feel about how you represent your offering. This brand communication includes everything you say and do—and everything you don't say or do. People and businesses need to get much more serious about taking responsibility for the conclusions the world draws about them and let go of first-person thinking for good. This approach is new, fertile ground to help distinguish you in the world. It's the difference between being seen as a self-absorbed brand and being seen as an inclusive brand.

This is what can happen when we are focused on the first person instead of the third person. Recently a business owner shared with me that he thought "fun should be an important part of his brand." This was a surprise since his business is a medical research company that tracks brain activity in animals through probes. In his mind, one of their core benefits is providing better systems to make getting to research analyses easier and faster than existing methods.

From his perspective, getting to the analysis is the "fun" part of what research is all about. While I'm glad he likes his job, I can promise you that fun is not at the core of this brand, and an outsider would be slightly mystified by the use of that word with their business. But this is an example of what can happen when you are *not* deeply and fully empathizing with those you serve.

This is a big deal, and I would like you to take a moment to contemplate what I am describing as it relates to how you present yourself and/or your business to the world. Do you present yourself in the context of, "Here is what you need to know about me"? Or, do you think about all the conclusions your audience will draw about you based on the sum of everything they can learn about you explicitly and implicitly? You need to deeply dive into the latter.

Many brands, especially on their websites, will go so far as to often just list their products or services for sale without any support of how they improve a life. If you look at the website of a medical practitioner, for example, there is almost always a list of the procedures they do. Every orthopedic surgeon will have a list of procedures they perform without much else: Arthroscopy, Cartilage Restoration, Joint Repair, Joint Replacement, Rotator Cuff Surgery, etc. This merely provides basic information without any inspiration.

This is also true and evident with that shortest of company messaging: the elevator pitch. Everyone recognizes the need for a rehearsed statement that quickly tells a prospect what a company does. Coming up with this pitch always seems to start with the question, "What do we tell prospects about why they should work with us?" The typical response most people and businesses choose is to identify what they think is important and then attempt to express it in an impressive way to inspire a transaction.

One problem with the elevator pitch is the instinct to reference familiar marketing terms that sound slick. But as this book has already detailed, those words have been used so many times that they have come to be viewed as boring and uninteresting at best, or downright manipulative at worst. As consumers, we've become desensitized to their intent because so many brands have destroyed what the words mean.

The other problem with elevator pitches is that they rarely invite questions or conversations. We expect the prospect—who is hearing the elevator pitch—to literally get off the elevator as soon as we are done with our 30-second spiel. They are notoriously close-ended descriptions of all the benefits we can possibly think of without inviting intrigue to inspire a set of questions to learn more. What we really want is to get a prospect interested enough to start a dialogue and maybe stick around for a full tour of the building.

That being said, let's deep-six the traditional elevator pitch as well. I'll show you a better way to share information about your offering that naturally flexes with time available and invites prospects to engage more deeply in the distinctive Pillars you introduce to them.

The challenge is to deeply empathize with the conclusions your audience will draw about you, based on everything they can see, hear, touch, or pick up on from every single explicit or implicit signal or message exhibited. We will go into in-depth examples of how to achieve this in the case studies later on in the book, but the thing to remember right now is that your customer understands more than you think. Humans are magnificent creatures capable of seeing beyond the surface. Understanding this about your customers will change the way you do business.

Empathizing may sound easy at first, especially since there are already a lot of sellers and marketers who will say, "We need to get inside the buyer's head." And, while some will do that to a degree, they usually fall right back into "here is what you need to know about me" mode. I am suggesting there is an entirely deeper level of empathy required. This is the practice of emotionally going into the state of being your buyer.

You are no longer you, working for the company you work for. You are your customer and deeply envisioning your brand experience, beginning from the very first exposure you would likely encounter. From that perspective, you start seeing your brand and business through your prospective customer's eyes, considering *every single detail* of what they can learn about you from every signal that will come their way. You will see and hear everything they would see as if you were encountering it for the very first time from their eyes, hearts, and minds.

You have to be very objective here. You are no longer a marketer or a seller. You are the person or family to whom you intend to be of service. You must deeply and objectively imagine how you would feel if you were them. What would you think of you if you were them? This is not a casual exercise to go into lightly where you allow your internal biases to remain and reign.

You are seeing yourself with fresh eyes, for the very first time. When a prospect is encountering a new proposition, they are closely looking at every single detail with a very scrutinizing lens because they are exploring benefits, but they are also scrutinizing for potential risks. When you are in that space, then you can start asking yourself the questions from their point of view.

If I were the prospect . . .

- Does my offering look like someone or something I would want to engage with immediately?
- Would I be immediately intrigued to learn more, based on that initial engagement?
- Do I immediately get the headline of what I am selling and feel inspired by it?
- Do I feel like I am getting a clear before and after picture of my life *without* the offering relative to my life *with* the offering?
- What potential risks might I be sensing about buying by what is being said in the pitch?
- What potential risks might I be sensing caused by what is *not* being said in the pitch?
- Am I being efficiently presented with logical Proof Points that convince me that the service or product will, in fact, make my life better?

Expedite is a new wound care product from Medtrition's product line that is coming to market with a core set of major advantages relative to competition. "Wound care," in this context, is another way of saying "bed sores," which are a terrible problem. The problem with the Expedite pitch was they were approaching the sale through their own perspective, with little consideration of how their approach would be perceived by the potential customer, who would be nurses and/or nutritionists at hospitals and long-term care facilities. There were multiple Mind Traps going on in this scenario, but the biggest was generic marketing speak with Feature Lister and OverExplainer Mind Traps.

The problem started on the first slide of their PowerPoint Pitch:

> *Pressure injuries take a serious toll on patients and health systems. But the current standard of care is not always enough. Now there's a way to do more. Now there's Expedite, the ready-to-drink medical food that delivers more.*

"Now there's a way to do more" is classic generic marketing hype. This intro was pandering and attempted to be too slick. After this slide, they introduced lists of disjointed features, and when they came to the technical aspects of how it worked, it was wordy and confusing without ever getting clearly to the payoff for the facility and caregivers. I see a lot of people wanting to build up to their punchline. That used to be more acceptable. Now you have to immediately convey why you matter, quickly tell me how you do it, and tell me how to buy.

We changed the entire approach in one sentence:

Expedite is a ready-to-drink, two-ounce wound-healing product that will revolutionize the way you nutritionally manage wounds and pressure injuries.

It was evident in this category that the standard approach has been in practice for so long that caregivers have become numb to how terrible the current state is. We wanted to take a fresh look and recognize the problem for each of the audiences affected—the patient and the caretaker. With the problem fresh, we highlighted the three primary advantages Expedite provides with a one-to-two-page explanation for each.

First, we solved a massive compliance issue by focusing on the small dose, ready-to-drink asset because competing products are time-consuming for the caretaker to mix and also often require the patient to drink uncomfortable amounts of liquid. Next, we proved how Expedite works faster and more effectively with natural ingredients, which also reduces the price and makes Expedite less expensive than the competition. The last point brought it back to how Expedite makes lives better for the three constituents involved and how their reputation and costs improve when wounds heal faster. It's a killer pitch that is immediately working well at the time this book is being drafted, easily increasing sales by over 30 percent.

Engaging with this intense empathy, then adjusting the approach to reflect what is needed to be inspired is the key to success. But empathy should not stop there. Doing the work to empathize with your customers and employees more gives you a better connection with what they want and expect from a direct relationship with your offering.

Focusing on empathy beyond the surface level will change every single interaction we have and revolutionize what we think of as professionalism. Our current standard of being professional also means cold, impersonal, and standoffish. I find it fascinating that we live in a world where everyone is craving greater connection, but we all stay apart based on an antiquated definition of what it means to convey respect.

The Human Touch

It's time to go a little further in defining "professional" to include a much greater component of what it means to be human. I have learned that few want to go first in creating the openness and vulnerability associated with rewarding engagement. I have also learned that those who go first in initiating meaningful engagement are almost always rewarded by a lasting relationship that stands the test of time.

The best and safest way I have found for "professionals" to initiate a deeper and more meaningful relationship is to risk being a little vulnerable about why you entered the profession you did. Tell them why you love what you do. Tell them why you love the company you work for with heartfelt gratitude. Buyers always begin sales transactions with their guard up because they think the salesperson cares more about money than making the customer happy—and, in fairness, that is probably true much of the time. The great thing about sharing the love of your product and what you do is that it is tremendously disarming and, in many cases, can inspire a customer to want to buy more. I find buyers like to help sellers be successful when they love what they do.

On a recent American Airlines flight, I heard a flight attendant do her pitch for the American Aadvantage credit card. I have over three million air miles, so I have heard this pitch many times.

I usually hear the standard, "This is a great opportunity to get 75,000 miles . . . blah, blah, blah," and I tune it out. But this time was different, and I was simply amazed by this attendant who did every single little sales detail right.

She first made sure we could see her talking and explained how there are actually two Aadvantage cards, and that she has both of them for good reason. Then she talked about why she loved these cards so much, how she used them, and what a great deal it was for her friends. She started with a love for what she was offering. With that foundation, she ended her general audience pitch and walked down the aisle slowly, chatting people up in the first few rows so that everyone on the flight would see that this was a different type of pitch. Many of the people in the subsequent rows all engaged in what was a conversation about why these credit cards were awesome and incurred no cost for the first year.

Next, when people expressed interest, she unfolded the trifold brochure and ripped off the one page that the client would keep for themselves and handed it to them . . . this effectively made her pitch an application in process, and she had a pen in hand. To each interested person, she asked them their frequent flier number and showed them the part of the form where they would add that piece of information. She also alleviated the possible complication of a prospect not having their number by writing down their seat number and then finding out the frequent flier number for them, which helped them complete the form during the flight. She also wrote down the seat number of every person who started the form and then made sure to follow up with all of them until she walked away with a completed form.

Because she had engaged so strongly from the beginning, nearly every row on that flight had someone completing an application. It was like nothing I had ever seen, so I had to ask her about it. She explained that she was one of the top performers at American and actually made more money from these credit card sales than she did as a flight attendant. She had even received free trips and had started training other attendants because of her success.

She explained that it all started with a love of the cards she was offering, followed by a process that naturally assumed the close. She paid attention to all the little details that might otherwise produce friction points that would reduce conversion. Did she love her cards? Yes! But she certainly did not come off as a superficial fanatic. Just her own positive experience with the cards was enough to make others want the same love and experience. If love can be found for a credit card, it can be found for anything!

By sharing what you love, you create an opening for the customer to follow with their own stories or what they were looking to find from your offering. This conversation starter will invite your customers to engage with you about your company and your products. The incremental benefit is that I find salespeople are happier as well and find greater satisfaction knowing they were a catalyst for greater expressions of joy. The reality is you have to give vulnerability to get vulnerability and great sellers have a knack for opening this in comfortable, bite-size chunks that allow buyers to comfortably join them.

Great salesmanship brings equal balance to three things that we teach in our training:
- Brand
- Core benefits
- The salesperson as an individual

In addition to selling features, with which most salespeople are already versed and comfortable, the brand component should convey a higher-level purpose with the introduction of a more meaningful before and after picture. The salesperson component is the opportunity to engage a customer as an ally and someone they are glad to know as someone who loves what they do or who they work for. As a salesperson, this may feel a little uncomfortable, but it is a skill that can be practiced, and the results are well worth the effort.

Bergdorf Goodman is a historic, luxury department store on Fifth Avenue in New York City. In the 20th century, it was famous for its mink department, featured as a favorite shopping destination for characters on the hit series *Sex in the City*. It currently offers exclusive brands like Loro Piana, Kiton, Brunello Cucinelli, John Lobb, Thom Brown, and Tom Ford. The typical clientele of Bergdorf Goodman is keenly aware of these brands and studiously follow fashion trends.

In an effort to create a greater connection with its patrons, we conducted an experiment. We split the Bergdorf Goodman salespeople into two groups. The control group continued to sell as they always had, which would normally involve approaching a customer with the question of, "Can I help you with anything today?" or, "Was there anything in particular you were looking for today?"

In the test group, we encouraged them to go shopping with the customer, employing the following mindset that they personalized: "I just love shopping at this store and there is something for everyone. I'd love to go shopping here with you." This tactic was immediately successful. Salespeople became friends with clients during the shopping process, building more personal and lasting client relationships, and sales increased 12 percent overnight. Having salespeople share and validate the love of fashion and shopping that is so evident in Bergdorf Goodman customers provided the connection needed to produce more sales.

I have observed that most salespeople and marketers with whom I come in contact are hesitant to make this kind of connection. Most feel more comfortable conveying the features of an offering and are less comfortable conveying the brand and sharing of themselves. The problem is when you focus on features, you commoditize your offering and fail to convey a deeper, richer meaning of how your offering may change a customer's life, and that a relationship with you could be inspirational to a richer fuller life.

When you are able to garner this kind of confidence, you are tapping into the core of what customers really want—connection.

CONSIDERATIONS...

- Be inspired by the **power of intense role-reversing empathy**.
- Seriously consider how you would **see the world in a third-person mindset** relative to a **first-person mindset**—not just a little, but all the way through every detail of the customer journey.
- What might you do differently if you were to **get serious about managing all of the conclusions your audience was making about you** rather than focusing on what you do using the language of what you thought you were supposed to say?

PART TWO

RISE

*Inspiring, Unifying, and Elevating Your Mission,
Your Brand, and All Aspects of Your Business*

The entire goal of this book is to help you rise both personally and professionally to your next level of success. First, we illuminated extremely foundational issues that could be holding you and your company back from reaching that success. And, while I think the insights on market trends are helpful and the Mind Traps will help you understand possible limitations to your current approach, without providing you a solution, there is little value in illumination. It's like a doctor who gives you a diagnosis but communicates no plans for treatment. It just doesn't make sense. Luckily, we have the answer and it has worked literally hundreds of times to help businesses achieve amazing levels of success.

I will be introducing you to the Rise Framework as the best means to counter the Mind Traps and present yourself in the most compelling light. Developing your Rise Framework will require you to rethink the assets at your disposal building on Intense Empathy described in the previous chapter. Before jumping to the Rise Framework, I want to give you some of my best tools that will further help you to distinguish yourself from the pack. There are three key approaches I love to use, including *painting your before and after picture*, which might be best described as the illumination of how you transform the lives of those you serve. We will also show you a down-and-dirty way to get real about your benefits and force you out of generic platitudes. Ultimately, we want to position you to *Claim the Top of Your Mountain* and gain the realistic opportunity to become the undisputed leader in your market segment. Then, with this lofty goal created, you'll learn how to give your proposition a complete inspirational reveal approach through the *Rise Framework* that equips you for dialogue in any setting.

This framework includes all the elements necessary to revolutionize your mindset, help you make goal-aligned, unifying decisions, and allow you to rise to previously only hoped-for heights.

CHAPTER FOUR

TACTICS TO CLAIM YOUR BEST SELF

———————

"Without communication, there is no relationship.
Without respect, there is no love. Without trust, there's
no reason to continue."
-The Buddha

Imagining and articulating the possibilities of the life of your customer before and after your offering came into their lives is an incredibly effective and essential process in creating your best brand and business. Again, it is absolutely critical to get out of your head and into the actual experience of your customer. Considering answers at both a functional and emotional level, ask yourself, "Before my offering came into their life, my prospect/client was experiencing _____. Now, with my offering in their life, they are experiencing _____." It's surprising to me how many companies are not clear how they are transformative to their customers because they are stuck in their transactional mindset instead of a relational one or are focused on what they do instead of why they matter.

We can easily see this illustrated through an example of a company I've worked with in the past. To the Association of Pool & Spa Professionals (APSP), everyone should want a pool or a hot tub. It's honestly hard to argue with that logic. I feel like I could safely bet that 10 out of 10 elementary school students would agree with the APSP, and really, most adults would too. But for many people, there are some glaring barriers.

APSP was stuck in a mindset of "Everyone should want a pool or spa; why don't they see that?"

Those on the fence in APSP's category have the means to purchase but are not convinced that the benefit-to-hassle ratio is sufficiently tilted to "benefit." After all, they will have to clean the pool, deal with chemicals, and spend extra time on maintenance. This understanding helps businesses move on from the mindset of feeling victimized to a position of knowing their real target is fence sitters who need to learn that new maintenance solutions substantially lower the hassle side of the equation shifting the balance of power to benefit and purchases.

To tilt that ratio, there are three necessary messaging strategies: 1) strengthen the benefit by highlighting additional and meaningful occasions for use; 2) highlight the emotional gains of use; 3) decrease the perceived hassle factor by explaining industry improvements made to reduce maintenance requirements.

For pools and spas, while the obvious benefit is fun, focusing on the added benefit of a better family life begins to change the equation. In addition, the pool's ability to facilitate greater emotional connections with friends and family helps a fence sitter see an even more intrinsic benefit and, perhaps most importantly, if the perceived hassle factor is reduced, many prospects will jump from doubters to buyers. We are changing the vision of the after picture to have a much higher benefit and much lower hassle visualization.

You can reach your customers better if you understand the following: they are looking for more meaning in their lives and purchases, they want to become their best selves, and they want to enhance their personal goals. With this information in mind, the next step is to start thinking about the details of who you are as a business and the customers you are trying to reach.

Getting to the Heart of Why You Matter

To help my clients get reconnected with their customers at the deepest level, I ask them to define the problem they **uniquely** solve for their customers. And who are those customers? The answers I receive generally have two flaws. First, they are not truly unique to them . . . others do it. Second, the answer is filled with generic marketing speak, which, as we have already established, sound like the right things to say rather than why they truly matter.

The struggle is to find the path to reconnect to the customer. For those comfortable doing it within the safe confines of the internal team, I may even go so far as to tell them to add profanity to their description. When you add profanity, you know you are no longer working on language you might attempt to use in your sales efforts and you are liberated to speak without inhibition. Second, when you are using expletives, it is usually because you are feeling more passionate and even angry about the topic. I want people to get animated about what the world and their clients would be missing if they were not part of it!

I recently worked through this process with a podcast company (JL). Here is the dialogue from our session:

> **Doug Harrison**: What is the problem you *uniquely* solve for your clients?

JL: We make podcasts for our clients who want to build a greater presence for themselves.

DH: Lots of people make podcasts . . . what do you do uniquely?

JL: We complete in-depth market analysis that allows our clients to understand how competitive their segment is.

DH: That's nice and helpful. Also, notice that you are still attempting to say the right thing rather than just going to your core connection. If you want, in a safe environment add some profanity to break out of the mode of feeling like you have to be saying the right things.

JL: We do great @&$# research to build podcasts to help people become more successful and then help them build their presence.

DH: Do you believe doing research is solving the core problem your client is seeking to accomplish?

JL: No, they are looking to build their recognized expertise while building a larger audience following them.

DH: Okay, so what are the things they require in order to accomplish that? Is the podcast a strategy or a tactic to that end?

JL: It would be a tactic.

DH: So, it would seem to me that if I am your client, my ultimate goal is to build a significant market presence that I could then monetize. I would be looking for a company that would help me efficiently build my digital presence where I would understand how my podcast content could be used in conjunction with other social media so that I could get the most bang for my buck and I would be smart about whether I should also be showing up to leverage that content either with Twitter, Instagram, Pinterest, TikTok, or LinkedIn. I would ideally want to understand how much investment I would need to make to connect to an actual ROI, which would require you to understand more about how my business model works.

My risk is that I spend a bunch of time and money to build podcasts with you and I have no idea if that is going to create an ROI. Your current business model is not helping me to create my full digital footprint, so am I making the most of this investment? Will 1,000 followers be a success, or do I need 100,000 followers?

JL: I understand we are focusing on podcasts because that is what we do and we like research, but that isn't necessarily tapping into what our clients actually need.

DH: Exactly. What you need to decide is what business you want to be in, what problem you uniquely want to solve in the world, and for what type of client so that your case approach is more repeatable and verifiable.

JL: We have to reconsider what business we are in.

DH: You have the opportunity to do so. You currently are in the business of doing podcasts for clients backed with strong research but that is very limiting relative to what your clients are seeking to accomplish. You could be in the business of helping successful people who want to strengthen their digital presence—so do it in the smartest, most cost-efficient way possible in the channels where they need to be with clarity of what their targets should be.

JL: We help awesome successful people who currently have a limited following to bring their talents to the world through podcasts and digital media. We show them how to leverage their content most effectively in the other digital media that best suits their business to grow their presence and quickly connect these efforts to ROI so they can grow at the right pace for themselves. Nobody does this as intelligently as we do.

Look at the difference from JL's last response to their initial response. The last response shows a company that has shifted from the process of what they do of making podcasts and doing research, which had limited awareness and consideration of their client to one that would be of far greater service and would dramatically increase both conversion and revenue per client.

Understanding your assets and how they emphatically fulfill unmet needs in the market is the first actionable step in the Rise process. This unique offering will become your Brand Promise, which will help you Claim the Top of your Mountain and will provide you with the direction you need to keep rising to a great brand with all the attributes great brands cultivate.

Brands Reflecting Back the Best of Who I Am

One of the concepts I am deeply attracted to can be described as the next generation of brand and business building. This concept is developed around the notion of brands being a reflection of "my best self." Here is how this works: every time I engage with a brand it triggers an emotional response. For example, driving a Ferrari elicits a different emotional response than if one drives, say, a minivan. The degree of impact will be influenced by the emotional response generated from engaging with the product or brand. While the Ferrari can make almost anyone feel powerful, the minivan can do the same thing for a person who has always dreamed of being a parent.

For me, there are three brands that elicit a strong emotional response. Coming from my background, they are products that help me see myself as the person I have strived my whole life to become. You will have your own based on your own personal experiences and values.

San Pellegrino is my favorite bottled water because I love the way it tastes when it is perfectly cold. It is a tiny premium indulgence I can have without ever feeling like I had to overspend to get it. I love the refreshing qualities it has, the green bottle, and even the label. I am so happy when I drink it because I feel like I'm living my best life.

Ermenegildo Zegna sport jackets are also my favorite. I love the fabrics they use because they fit me perfectly. Perhaps what I love the most is that every time I put on one of their jackets, I feel more successful and confident in any situation. Whether I am in a social or business environment, wearing this jacket makes me feel special because it makes me look great, and its premium price point gives me an exclusive experience.

My BMW 840i convertible is simply beautiful, and I love it. There are so many things I love about it: the paint color that somehow magically mixes blue and black together, the tan leather interior, and the versatility of the engine. I also love that I can feel the sun and wind when I put the top down, and I love that I feel like a more successful person who has done well in business when I drive it. Not only do I feel more successful, but I also look successful because it sends a signal to others that I have accomplished a lot in my life.

When I experience each of these brands, they connect with me in a very personal and meaningful way, and when I am engaged with them, I truly feel like the best version of myself. I feel elevated and more fulfilled. Think about the products that inspire similar feelings in you. Maybe they are sustainable products that align with your value of being kind to the earth. Maybe they are nostalgic products from your past that have maintained their quality and help you feel connected to your family.

What is remarkable to me is that, in my entire lifetime, I have identified only three brands that have evoked a deep emotional response in me. I believe the reason for this is that business is dominated by a transactional mindset. There is an inherent lack of empathy for those we serve, and the current standard for excellence is producing functional quality and customer service.

I suggest that all the products on your "best self" list come from businesses that have a relational mindset, which are focused on creating truly inspired illumination and connection at the highest levels (either that, or they just perfectly nailed the product offering). I believe that brands and businesses whose offerings encourage customers to feel and be their best selves are revolutionizing what distinction means, and it will be the destination all businesses strive for as the bar of customer satisfaction continues to rise.

One of my current entrepreneurial ventures is a wellness business. With my friend Sandy Rasque, we created Smart Swapping, based on the idea of replacing not-so-good meals, mindsets, and movements with ones that better serve them. We give health advisors and trainers a platform where they can nurture new habits that their clients will want to choose for a lifetime. It is the first wellness program to replace sacrifice with abundance, because sacrifice is not a sustainable choice many people will make for the long haul. As an example, our foods focus on delivering twice the flavor with half the calories of their traditional counterparts. If we can replace feelings of deprivation with abundance, we can support sustained wellness. It works wonderfully.

The target Sandy and I have set for this business is not to just have great recipes that replace the problematic ones, or to have great new habit-building tools. Our plan is to be the destination where people who desire wellness go to experience the best of themselves and live the life they want to live, surrounding themselves with others who are doing the exact same thing. We are very intentional about articulating that this is a community and program built around unconditional love for each other. This is the consistent thread across everything I do. We all rise together.

People struggling with weight loss, for example, are incredibly hard on themselves and one of the principal ways they fall off the weight loss trail is through familiar indulgence that reminds them of their failure yet again. One slip becomes another cheat and then the self-criticism jumps in where they accuse themselves of yet another failed attempt, which makes them feel as if all is lost. For people who have tried to lose weight for a long time, this is a never-ending cycle that's hard to break away from.

With Smart Swapping, we are clear that weight loss, despite all the media and advertising that says otherwise, is not a straight line to success and that perfection is neither expected nor realistic. Because of our ongoing engagement tools, we can tell when these individuals quietly slip off the rails and we can quickly course correct and bring them back. Because we have aligned and tracked the new habits nurtured with their advisor, we can always point to progress, even when slipups occur.

By basing our process on love, we moved from being a functional wellness product to a brand and destination where people can find the best of themselves and be around others who are also inspired to find the best of themselves.

When businesses operate with that mindset—to continually deliver love and acceptance and inspiration through experiences and programs—something truly magical is created. When you do this with your business, you will add to this magic and provide your customers with a new, brighter vision of their future. It also attracts a higher level of talented employees who are unified in wanting to be part of something bigger than themselves.

CONSIDERATIONS...

- How good of a job are you doing at **painting the before and after picture** of the lives of the people you serve with your proposition embedded in it?
- Consider if **redefining the business** you are in might better connect you to the needs your target is experiencing. **Get raw** in the benefits you can provide.
- What can you do to be the place **where people come to experience the best of themselves?**

CHAPTER FIVE

CLAIM THE TOP OF YOUR MOUNTAIN

———————

"People do not decide to become extraordinary.
They decide to accomplish extraordinary things."
-Sir Edmund Hillary

In March 1953, after climbing nearly 29,000 feet on the world's highest-reaching mountain, Edmund Hillary and his guide, Tenzing Norgay, faced one more obstacle—a 12-meter, nearly vertical rock face—before reaching the top of Mount Everest and claiming the title of the first to ever reach its summit. "Wedging himself in a crack in the face, Hillary inched himself up what was thereafter known as the Hillary Step."[3] Once at the top, he threw down a rope, pulled up Norgay, and the climbers became the first to stand on the very top of the world.

You are already working to succeed and reach your goals. You would not be reading this book otherwise. With the right focus, your goals can become even higher and you will be able to rise to meet them. One of the things that surprises people when we work with them is that we spend little time focusing on competitors in the early stages of an engagement.

A great point my dear friend, Dr. James Taylor, would reinforce with our clients was to focus on *distinction* rather than *differentiation*. When you focus too much on your competitors you place yourself in a reactionary mode and, from the very beginning, you put yourself in a position of inferiority, which is what differentiation is about. But in reality, when you discover your unique offering to the world built on extreme empathy, it creates competitive advantage because you are operating in a mode of being of the highest purpose and service beyond what competitors are doing.

When you pay too much attention to competitors, I find you start trying to do things like they are rather than doing what is best for those you choose to serve. You will be able to *Claim the Top of Your Mountain* when you focus on your purpose. This means finding and claiming all the required products, messaging, partnering, and culture opportunities to distinctively *own* your space. I like to revisit the competitive landscape after I work through the Rise process and then adjust if needed. However, I have to tell you, when we do this process well, we have something that wins because your competitors don't have this.

I am involved with a company called Events.com. As you might tell by its name, Events.com is about all things events, but primarily makes its money by event organizers paying a fee to use the Events.com platform to manage ticketing and registration. A strength of the brand is the Events.com name and its expanding presence in the industry. However, they have a competitor, which shall remain nameless, that focuses only on race events.

The competitor only does races, so they focus on doing every little thing right to message, build case studies, find the right partners, and have the best technology to serve races. They focus only on that target to build their presence. That competitor has Claimed the Top of the Racing Event Mountain and now every time Events.com comes up against them, they know they are in for a battle.

Smaller and midsize companies I help support generally aren't clear what Mountain they are seeking to own. Most focus on a skill or capability they do well and they emphasize that: "We make great pies," or, "We have smart technology," or, "We do quality construction." All of these are what you do, but they are not why you matter. There are many companies that likely do much of what you do. Going deeper into recognizing how you incrementally matter requires a deeper commitment to defining a purpose that aligns with what your customers seek.

The Traits of a Great Brand

After working with hundreds of businesses and brands, we identified four qualities that great brands know with clarity about themselves which have helped them remain at the Top of their Mountain:

- Mastery
- Scarcity
- Value Proposition
- Consistency

These strengths permeate every aspect of great companies because they inspire buyers to want to purchase their products. Employees are also naturally drawn to want to work with the company and feel happy once they are there . . . most importantly, these are the employees you would want to have working for you because they share your company values. Operations get built to deliver on this vision making your entire organization into a powerful symphony.

Mastery

Great brands are masters in their category. They have gone through the process of identifying their unique assets and how they fulfill an important unmet need in the market. They understand how they best serve their ideal customers, and they pursue distinction in the market. They Claim the Top of Their Mountain and deliver on a clear promise to the market, which forces every other company to navigate around them.

One excellent example of this is T-Mobile. Remember when Verizon basically owned the cellphone space? Their famous "Can you hear me now?" campaign focused on their commitment to providing coverage everywhere. When new T-Mobile CEO John Legere started his position, he knew they couldn't match Verizon on the coverage front, so he didn't try. Instead, he became known as the rebel CEO and balked at every tradition and rule cellphone companies had in place which aligned with the T-Mobile persona.

He made contracts more flexible, focused on prepaid phones, separated the phone from the service, and established T-Mobile as the "un-carrier" with the mantra "Only T-Mobile breaks the rules to break you free." With their accompanying leather-clad, motorcycle-riding advertisements, their rebel campaign increased T-Mobile customers by 22 million in just two years. T-Mobile created their own Mountain.

Scarcity

Great brands have the elemental quality of exclusivity . . . there is some unique access point. In some cases, this is actual scarcity from insufficient inventory or inventory made to feel inadequate to serve the greater demand. Fashion retailer Hermes would rather burn extra inventory if they have it rather than discount it. This reflects how seriously they take scarcity as a brand value.

Even Coca-Cola has some qualities of scarcity. When you drink a Coca-Cola relative to a store brand, some of the happiness and emotional refreshment they have reinforced over thousands of impressions comes through to make that experience more special. And, of course, for companies like Lamborghini, whose product offering is only in the financially feasible realm for a small percentage of the population, price can also be used to reinforce scarcity. But scarcity can also happen when a brand connects with customers and conveys their understanding of customer needs and values. The way you present yourself in a true, meaningful, and distinct way causes scarcity too.

Value Proposition

Great brands have a clear set of deal terms that both the company and the customer are completely aligned upon. The value proposition is inherently the sum of everything a company will give a customer in exchange for the money paid for it. Amazon may have the strongest value proposition on the planet today. They will make nearly everything you could possibly want available in an instant, and then deliver it quickly, sometimes within the hour, and often without a delivery charge. Walmart has a similar value proposition, but with a greater emphasis on price and the retail environment. Later on, I'll show you how to define your value proposition and easily convey your core values and associated offering with your customers.

Consistency

Great brands produce a consistent conclusion across all their touchpoints. Many businesses actually avoid consistency in driving the same conclusion for fear of being boring and redundant. Consistency means that every time I encounter your proposition, I draw the same conclusion. McDonald's is a clear example in this category. No matter where you are in the world, McDonald's is going to feel like McDonald's and taste like McDonald's. They systematize everything, down to the growing of their own potatoes for their French fries, to make a consistent experience.

Consistency is vital. The factor most likely to cause you to believe something is true is the frequency you hear it. When you talk about a variety of dimensions in your communications, they can easily become overwhelming. People want to make a clear connection as to why you matter. The human mind is designed to efficiently draw conclusions to help manage life. Experts estimate that as much as 95 percent of our thoughts are unconscious because we have established meaning or responses over a series of encounters.[4]

I know when I turn the wheel in my car clockwise that I will turn right. I no longer need to contemplate this decision. It just happens and that frees my consciousness to go explore other things that might require greater attention or might have greater risk to my survival. Consistency, then, is an amazing tool that creates an emotional connection with customers. After having so many consistent, positive interactions, the decision to engage will become decision-less and automatic. This gives a business powerful emotional protection that will require a competitor to make a major lift to dislodge.

Consistency becomes even more important since most sellers do not realize that every incremental point they try to make has an exponential impact on the number of mental calculations a prospect has to consider . . . in other words, buyers don't consider each of your selling points in isolation. In their effort to avoid risk, prospects consider each point you make in combination with every other point to assess if they could logically coexist.

For example, if I tell you that you are getting my dedicated top talent to serve your account (message 1) and also tell you that you'll be receiving the highest quality (message 2), those two messages logically make sense together, so the prospect is likely to continue. If you add a third message that you are the lowest cost (message 3), then the entire thing is likely to fall apart because lowest price does not make sense with senior talent and highest quality based on past experiences. This is known as cognitive dissonance, which is a well-established psychological principle, and a prospect may bail unless you can quickly prove how you distinctly accomplish this combination.

Keep in mind that when there were two messages, the prospect's mind had to do four mental calculations they were not even aware were happening to compare each message with its connected plausibility with the other message. When the third was added, nine mental calculations were required. Add a fourth message, and the prospect now has 16 mental calculations, and the confusion and sense of being overwhelmed begins to set in. Either inconsistency between messages or an overwhelming number of messages can trigger the conclusion that the entire proposition is a lie, and they reject the offer with the benefit of keeping their money in their pocket and feeling like a smarter shopper.

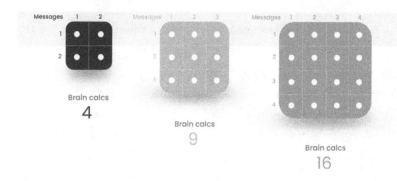

Introducing the Rise Framework

All of the best brand traits should be working together to make sure the messaging is focused and does not overwhelm a customer. We created the Rise Framework to connect these factors and help companies reap the benefits of an organized, focused, solid strategy. There are six key benefits to following the Rise Framework:

1. **We reduce the marginal cost of effective communication and raise the marginal cost for direct competitors.** When it is more singularly easy to remember why you matter, it costs less to create that conclusion. Competitors will struggle and need to spend more to attempt to dislodge the conclusion.

2. Branding provides **a foundational Promise to which all future endeavors** must align. A good Promise should last a lifetime. A good Brand Promise will keep you from wasting your time on extensions or pursuits that will be a distraction and confusing to your purpose rather than accretive. This keeps operations focused toward delivering core benefits.

3. **Consistency** is the best predictor of brand inoculation, authenticity, and transcendence. Consistency around a great brand is not boring: it can be comforting to make

a repeat purchase decision. Activities undertaken by the business should help reinforce the conclusion of the Promise while still expanding the ways in which the Promise is delivered.

4. **Every message must invoke the brand value equation, and every exposure to a product—message, observation, and use—is a brand message**. As a result, employees, influencers, customers, and environment are crucial to the brand messaging process.

5. **Scarcity and desire are the best friends of margin**. I will pay more when FOMO exists (fear of missing out).

6. **A great brand and business framework helps attract the talent you want.** The values of the company should no longer be separated from the values of service. Employees want to be inspired by working for a company that has a greater purpose where all functions are orchestrated to serve that end.

The benefits of the Rise Framework have been realized in every company we have worked with who use it as a guide to maneuver through the ins and outs of their daily work. I know that it can work for you too. Time to begin.

CONSIDERATIONS...

- What are the **elements that might be able to come together for you to "Claim the Top of Your Mountain?"** These are the things you **uniquely** possess and deliver.

- **Complete a self-assessment** to identify what you are a **master** at providing, what is inherently **scarce** about what you provide, what are the clear deal terms or

value proposition of your solution, and how are you **consistently** presenting this to your target audience. Do this for your own internal workings. This does not have to be customer facing.

- Get ready! The next chapter is going to start revealing how you can **construct your own Rise Framework to own your Mountaintop**.

CHAPTER SIX

THE RISE FRAMEWORK

"The loftier the building, the deeper must the foundation be laid."
-Thomas à Kempis

The Rise Framework is the organizational structure companies need in order to connect every aspect of their business around a cohesive strategy that enables their unique product offering to create meaningful connections with their customers. For this book, I want you to have all the tools and steps you need to build your own Rise Framework and help you Claim the Top of Your Mountain. I want to be very clear that this process is substantially different from what has been done historically. What we are creating will directly resonate with your customers and prospects in the real world. It will be simple, it will be clear, and it will be powerful.

We will be strong and definitive about a formula and position for your brand that you can use right away. It will effectively direct future messaging and business activities, while also encompassing product composition and presentation. While reading about this process will obviously be different than having our team come and analyze your business for you, it is my great desire that you and your company can take the information from this book, realize your contribution to the world, connect with your audience, and take your business to the next level.

Most organizations I have encountered silo their organization around the specific roles of Sales, Marketing, Operations, Accounting, and Human Resources. But for any of these roles to be successful, they must work together cohesively around a unified vision. When I began doing this work years ago, my original intent was to drive branding and messaging from the marketing perspective. What has become clear over time is that this work functions best when it permeates every aspect of the business.

Bringing this all together in one powerful approach also aligns with this new world in which our customers and clients are seeking greater depth of connection. Everything must come together like a wonderfully conducted orchestra to translate into a reality in which the customer experience reflects the truth of why you exist. In a world of transparency, if all of your orchestra sections are not in sync with each other, there is a much greater possibility that the off-notes will be heard and amplified.

The impact of this framework is truly transformational on companies, which you will easily see in the case studies presented later in the book. This framework does not produce mere little tweaks, but major wonderful changes for businesses that are at the same time new and familiar. These changes are completely attainable because they build on the core qualities you already possess or are within reach; they're just enhanced in a way that gives you a clear direction, like the North Star, to continue your journey forward.

There is another major benefit to this structure. So often, brands write a narrative that presents themselves one way to the world. Brands and businesses need to branch out and realize this one way doesn't work for all their customers or employees. They will have varying degrees of time to spend with you. Some will only tune in briefly while others will seek a deeper immersion before committing to buy. Through the Rise Framework, you will learn how to present your offering whether those prospects have thirty seconds or thirty minutes to learn more about you.

In this process, you will also incorporate sales, targeting, operations and culture into the mix. It involves a four-tier structure that at the highest level begins with the Promise. Under the Promise are the Pillars, Proof Points, and Power Plant that serve as the supporting construct through which everything flows up and down. Together these categories work together to make that cohesive, connected message and set of coordinated actions that will help you rise in your business pursuits and goals.

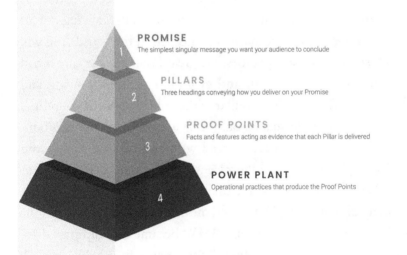

PROMISE
The simplest singular message you want your audience to conclude

PILLARS
Three headings conveying how you deliver on your Promise

PROOF POINTS
Facts and features acting as evidence that each Pillar is delivered

POWER PLANT
Operational practices that produce the Proof Points

The Promise

The highest level of expression for your offering is the Promise. This is the simple, singular, but powerful conclusion about the unique offering you bring to the world and how you are going to connect with your customer to deliver its full value and potential. The Promise is your connection to your audience. For Tiffany & Co., the Promise is *Love*. For Walmart, the Promise is *Value for Every Part of Your Life*. For Amazon, the Promise is *Everything You Want in One Place, and Delivered to You Fast*. Coca-Cola's Promise is *Happiness*. The Ritz-Carlton's Promise is *Ladies and Gentlemen Serving Ladies and Gentlemen*.

These Promises are the Mountain summit. Each of these brands seeks to connect with their customers in a personal way, and these Promises help these successful companies deliver true value.

While simply stated, the Brand Promise contains nuance and detail to encapsulate the scope and value of your business. Above all, the Promise must be *true* of what you offer, *meaningful* to those you seek to serve, and *distinct* relative to competition. A great Promise requires all three and it becomes the rallying cry for why businesses exist—to be what is needed in the world. You will notice some other key qualities to a great Promise. They are broad enough to support growth and evolution to keep growing and improving. They are also familiar without being generic sounding.

Quality or Performance cannot be a Promise! I chuckle about this a little because I have worked with two car companies who each thought their Brand Promise was Performance. The problem with Performance is that it actually means many different things to many different people. It could mean speed, agility, or even longevity of the engine. In the end BMW became the "ultimate driving machine" and Audi is about "intelligently inspired design." A great Promise, like these, also needs to align with a deep emotional desire on the part of the intended audience.

When I work with clients on discovering their Brand Promise, I have them seek the following characteristics and answer the following questions:

- Is it *true* of what I do, is it *meaningful* to those I seek to serve, and is it *distinct* relative to competition?
- Does it have depth and purpose?
- Does it avoid generic marketing speak?
- Does it invite customers to ask, "How do you do that?"
- Are we helping to build on the existing assets we possess to further serve the unmet needs of the category where we can best exist and become the best we can be?
- Does the Promise effectively headline the underlying framework? (I'll talk more about this later.)
- Does the Promise come with a purity that is very intentional to be of service?

That is the power of a great Promise. A short phrase can inspire a whole bunch of conclusions without saying more, while inviting a deeper conversation to elaborate your purpose and proposition. The Promise becomes the short word or phrase a buyer or prospect shares with others. We want to control the words our audience says about us to the greatest extent possible.

A great Promise will be inspirational to everyone when they learn about it, and customers will be drawn to want to be part of it, because it represents a state of being bigger than ourselves. A great Promise is being part of the best of who and what we want to seek in the world. In today's current environment where there is so much noise, confusion, and loneliness, wherever we can find places that represent something bigger than ourselves, something that is real, meaningful, and connected, that place will be deeply attractive.

Supporting the Promise are the Pillars, Proof Points, and Power Plant that all sequentially flow into each other. Part of avoiding falling into generic sales speak is to incorporate sequentially the supporting tiers that serve to validate your Promise. By presenting logically organized, understandable, and credible evidence, you deliver your Promise. Pillars could be considered the organizing construct or headline areas that align under the Promise.

The Pillars, Proof Points, and Power Plant

These supportive structures are the foundation you need on your journey to Claim the Top of Your Mountain. They also provide the verbiage to relay your value proposition to prospects that will replace the standard overdone elevator pitch. We have had a lot of successes defining the Pillars around three territories, which will become more apparent with the case studies. While we start with these three categories in mind, they act as guidelines more than rules. We adjust them depending on the brand, the level of customer involvement, and the nature of the offering.

- *The Product Benefits Pillar*: What is special about how you provide what you do, how it fills a market need, and most importantly, how it is inherently true? Go deep with it to build out the Proof Points and Power Plant and then develop a Pillar headline that summarizes all your wonderful points in a unique way.

- *The Emotional Pillar*: Detail how the process or product you provide affects your customers' emotions when they engage with your offering. Build out this section as well with Proof Points and Power Plant that show how your company will accomplish supporting your customers in becoming their best selves.

- *The Relationship Pillar*: Make this Pillar all about the connection you seek to have between your brand/company and the customer. Find the intersection between what you are looking for and can deliver now or in the near future to what they are seeking. Again, populate these details into the Power Plant and Proof Points as makes sense, and then ladder them up to create the Pillar Heading conclusion. This Pillar in particular will drive the scarcity of your offering.

Combined, these become a complete construct for engagement. Another great aspect of having three Pillars is that it is a manageable number a prospect can keep organized in their brain.

The Proof Points can be a variety of things that act as evidence that the Pillar is true and believable. For example, if a Pillar was "We are the Perfect Extension to your Team," then the Proof Points will need to show proof through process and examples to validate the Pillar. The Power Plant that supports the Proof Point is the Operational Systems and Culture that make all this possible. This can get into hiring processes, training, operational systems, supply chain, manufacturing, technical advantages, etc. The Power Plant produces the Proof Points that support the Pillars that empower the Promise. And in doing this you have developed a framework that allows you to comfortably tell the story of why you matter to the world in any amount of time.

If you are literally on an elevator, describe your Promise and Pillars in just 30 seconds or less. If these headings are done well, it will invite conversation in ways the elevator pitch never has. The answers to those questions, if you have a few more minutes, are summary descriptions of the Pillars. Have half an hour? Describe the Pillars in greater detail and convey the Proof Points. And if you have a really interested prospect, you can go through everything. At each level, your messaging will invite engagement that leads to conversion because your prospects will get why you matter.

You can envision this process as building a case of overwhelming evidence that you are the real deal and that your offering is cohesive, relatable, and understandable. There is a headline Promise that will speak to the emotional impact the customer wants to receive with the level of information that can be unpacked in layers depending on their time and desire to learn more.

The case studies that follow will illustrate the Rise Framework in action. After going through this process of building the Rise Framework, you will be better equipped to move forward. What we typically hear from clients is, "This is what we have always wanted to convey about ourselves, but never knew how." We have had several clients brought to tears, they were so happy and relieved to articulate with confidence why and how they mattered. This language will feel both familiar and foreign because it is a new way of articulating your offering and it does take a little getting used to.

One of my favorite ways of testing to see if we have it right is if our clients start using the language naturally during the first week or two because they are drawn to it. This is the single greatest validation that it is working. Leadership will feel like it is the best of themselves, and they naturally start using it because it feels good. If it feels forced, then the messaging needs to be revisited. Done well, it starts to feel like a dear friend you have been seeking your entire life, but never knew existed.

This is the process. These are the solutions. These are ways to break through and serve the world in unprecedented ways. Business and life become more beautiful and easier with these revelations actively in play every day of your business. And when you reach that point, you'll know that you have risen.

CONSIDERATIONS...

- Get ready to **replace your current elevator pitch with the Rise Framework** as a means of moving from a closed-ended description of what you do into an introduction that inspires connection.

- How often could you benefit from an approach that allows you to **present your offering in 20 seconds, two minutes, 20 minutes, or two hours,** depending on the time availability and interests of your prospect?

- **Consider replacing mission statements and company value statements** that often fall into generic language **with the Rise Framework,** which will represent a singular approach that will pull all aspects of sales, marketing, operations, and culture together in one cohesive package.

CHAPTER SEVEN

BEWARE OF UNINTENDED RISK ESCALATORS

———————————

"Is the glass half empty, half full, or twice as large as it needs to be?"

-Author Unknown

Before we proceed, a word of caution. Even if your framework messaging is on point, and you are working hard to Claim the Top of Your Mountain, there are *Exponential Risk Escalators* that can work against you and your business. You need to be aware and beware of these factors.

As you read through the case studies, you'll notice I frequently talk about risks we are mitigating in the Rise Framework, e.g., Sellers Sell Benefits, But Buyers Choose to Buy or Not Based on Risk; Marketers Play to Win, But Buyers are First Playing Not to Lose. The big risk factors for sales and marketing are all the big and small, explicit and implicit details often not noticed by the seller, but definitely recognized by the prospect.

This is the challenge of being in your business every day. When you are busy getting the proposal out, ordering the inventory, or writing the sales copy, you are in a get-it-done mode. Over time you become numb to the risk factors of working with you. The weaknesses are bad enough in their own right but are even more problematic because of the magnified conclusions they generate for prospective customers. These weaknesses are gaps that, when noticed by prospective customers, turn into Exponential Risk Escalators, and really hurt your business.

Let's start with our first official case study—my company. Our market research and consulting company did very high-quality work and businesses relied on our advice to make decisions that would impact hundreds of millions or billions of revenue in some cases. We were very thorough in our analysis and interpretation and were highly sought out and trusted.

Knowing how easy it is to get lost in day-to-day work, I hired a consultant friend to speak to our clients and see what they had to say about us under conditions of anonymity. We received the feedback we expected in terms of the quality of our work and impact we had on their business. There was one major surprise I had not anticipated, but it was obvious as soon as I heard it. The feedback was that our reports looked dated. The look and feel were starting to look old and the reports were too long and too dense. The market had moved to "less is more" on a page with the emphasis on beautifully conveying conclusions rather than depth of explanation.

You might think our reports looking dated was probably not a big deal—some might not even worry about it. But there was an Exponential Risk Escalator. Our outdated look and feel caused our clients to wonder if our project methods and analytics were also getting outdated. Even worse, there was a risk that over time our clients might become embarrassed to show our work and could possibly stop using us because it made them look out of sync with market standards. Even if they believed our analysis and conclusions were superior to competitors who had shinier deliverables, it didn't matter. It could still affect their reputation.

Oftentimes, it is not what we say specifically that is the issue, but rather what is implied. With this particular issue, we implied it didn't matter that our customers would be seen as working with an outdated company. Needless to say, we upgraded this skill immediately and turned it into a strength once we became aware of it.

Let's look at another example that you might recognize from several experiences throughout your life. We were invited by a Mercedes Benz dealership to have a look at their customer experience and what they might improve. We immediately saw dust bunnies in one cluttered corner of the showroom. The personnel walked by each day and never thought a second about it because it had been there for a long time. However, this had an Exponential Risk Escalator impact on customers.

The underlying feeling was, "If they are so sloppy that they can't even take care of their showroom, they will probably also be sloppy in taking care of me and my car." Wow! A few dust bunnies could carry that degree of impact on a conclusion. With Mercedes Benz being a luxury brand, this was not the image they wanted their customers to remember about them. It had just been there so long that it became invisible to their eyes.

We also worked with jewelry maker Cartier. One of our problematic findings with their stores was the security guard posted at the front door. While this might make the company feel more secure, what message was being sent to prospects entering the store? Was the armed guard their welcoming committee? We learned that the guard was, in fact, an Exponential Risk Escalator, making some potential customers not want to enter the store.

A fierce-looking guard standing watch signals an unfriendly and even foreboding environment inside which everyone is more defensive, and a fun or pleasant shopping experience becomes unlikely. This is obviously an issue since this is the exact opposite feeling you seek when buying exquisite jewelry in a spirit of celebration and fun. They moved the guard and sales went up.

Deficiencies can also be the things you don't say or do. This is particularly important to make sure you are covering the most essential fundamentals of why individuals buy in your category. I can't tell you how many times I have run into new healthy foods that are so busy telling you why they are good for you that they forget to say we taste good. Or products that are so focused on conveying their features that they forget to say they back them with great customer support. This is why it is so imperative to operate in the third person, imagining how your prospect will feel from every sense they can learn about your offering.

We worked with a solar company who was using a sales pitch that was fast and aggressive, intended to convey strength and efficiency. Instead, they were leaving an impression of having a wham-bam approach so the company could go make money on the next project. Prospects wondered if their culture was harsh with high turnover. If this all resulted in shortcuts and future problems, the decision would look bad to their CEO for suggesting solar in the first place. Not the desired conclusion at all!

Every solar company has their portfolio of projects. The gap is how does the prospect know you are going to do their project effectively? It's great you have done projects for everyone else, but the prospect wants assurance that their particulars will not be overlooked. You don't want your prospects walking away asking questions like this. What you communicate about your offering should set their minds at ease.

We helped this company recognize a proprietary process for making sure they were maximizing benefits for the client given the particulars of their property layout and energy needs. We also crafted how they would present the project team the client would be working with. We highlighted their expertise and experience, but also that they were nice people the client would enjoy working with. We also built in the story for longitudinal support so they could have confidence they would be taken care of for a lifetime. Guess what happened . . . sales conversions went up!

There are so many places and ways this can play out. Worn furniture in a hotel lobby produces an Exponential Risk Escalator. A guest could worry, "The linens on my bed might be dirty!" and they may enter their room with the expected feeling of grossness. A contract that has language that sounds like the seller is more concerned for themselves than the customer also produces an Exponential Risk Escalator. A potential client might feel, "I am being asked to enter a relationship where my counterpart is always going to attempt to cheat me for their own advantage, so I will always need to be on guard. That can be exhausting . . . do I really need a relationship like that?"

All propositions are filled with dozens if not hundreds of details that can lead to Exponential Risk Escalators. These are particularly hard to spot when you are in your own head because we become numb to our environments while prospects are seeing us for the first time.

You can do nine things right, but the one thing you do less than right will be penalized substantially because of this dynamic. That is because buyers are first operating to avoid risks instead of seeking benefits. Sellers are selling the three shiny apples they like to emphasize about their product, but buyers are looking at the whole basket of apples. When they can find a bad apple—even if it is a little one—it causes them to wonder how many other bad apples there are that they cannot see. If they see one or two, chances are good others will be present. Sellers have insufficient appreciation for how good it feels for a prospect to say no. When prospects say no, they have avoided the risk of wasting their money on something they might regret later, and it feels good to keep their money in their pocket.

Gap	Exponential Risk Escalator
Outdated report style	Outdated statistical models and processes. Embarrassment to clients that could result in lost relationships.
Showroom dust bunnies	Sloppy process management and service capabilities. Risk of hassles, time wasted, and potential damage to my car.
Omnipresent armed guard	Tense showroom environment. Guilty until proven innocent. Dampens fun and desire to celebrate what should be some of one's favorite purchases!
"Solar is good. We do solar."	Doesn't mean clients will like working with you. You will focus on speed over client's interests. We could have problems near-term and long-term. This becomes a risk that can make the direct client look bad to their boss. Safer to say no.

Seller-sided contracts	"I will always have to be on guard. Do I really want to engage with someone who always puts their self-interests first? Maybe look else-where."
What are yours?	What risks do they exponentially escalate to?

It is nearly impossible not to become insulated in our own businesses. We lose perspective of what it is like to be a prospect experiencing every little detail of explicit and implicit information your prospects can determine about your offering from all their senses.

Find someone you can trust who can help bring you that perspective. "There is gold in them hills" when you can find the gaps and replace them with advantages that can enhance conversion. And when you do, shoot me a note, and let me know what you did. I will congratulate you and it will make my day!

CONSIDERATIONS...

- Remember, **sellers sell on benefits, but buyers are first screening to avoid risks.**
- **Take a fresh look at your offering** with the lens of **risks you might be presenting either implicitly or explicitly.** Consider how these might create Exponential Risk Escalators.
- **What will you do or say to eliminate these risks** and replace them with benefits?

PART THREE

RISE IN ACTION

Inspiring Case Studies Leveraging the Rise Framework

This section presents some compelling case studies of the clients we have helped using the Rise Framework. Each case study is based on a single company or individual and is focused on their most prominent Mind Trap. The case studies focus on small and midsized businesses; however, the same approach can be applied to companies of any size. You won't see any mention of Amazon, Microsoft, or Google here because I wanted the content to be relatable for small and midsize companies.

Each case study begins with a deeper explanation of the particular Mind Trap. You may be tempted to read only those case studies associated with your Mind Traps, but I can promise you will find value in reading all of them because the same Rise Framework largely solves all Mind Traps. In other words, recognizing a Mind Trap is important because it helps you see why you need to change, but the same Rise Framework can serve all Mind Traps.

Working with the varying degrees of comfort our clients felt in sharing their stories and supporting elements, I included as many details as possible to help you fully understand the Mind Traps and see the process that helped companies and individuals overcome them.

Each of the case studies covers the following . . .

- **Mind Trap Description and Associated Issues:** Mind Traps inhibit people and/or organizations from finding their unique, value-added benefits.
- **Natural Habitats:** Some Mind Traps are more or less prevalent within specific types of companies and industries.
- **The Before Picture:** A summary of the state of affairs for the client prior to building and launching the Rise Framework.
- **The After Picture using the Rise Framework:** Identifying the Top of the Mountain for the client covering the Promise, Pillars, and supporting Proof Points. We reveal the recognized and unrealized assets and opportunities we leveraged to build their Rise Framework.
- **Target Impact:** Clarity of how targeting evolved.
- **Culture Shift:** A strong, clear, and organized business and value proposition unifies a workforce increasingly seeking meaning and purpose.
- **Client Comments:** Reflections of those we served.

My hope is that in sharing these stories, you will be able to better understand the Mind Traps while gaining more insight into the process of creating a Rise Framework. I also hope that you can see yourself or your business in these cases, and that it will give you hope and inspiration to take action and Rise yourself. Keep in mind that this is hard to do for yourself, particularly if you have not done it before. Reach out to us and see if we can help!

CHAPTER EIGHT
THE COPY CATTER

Slipping into the **Copy Catter** Mind Trap occurs when you are not clear in conveying what you *uniquely* solve for your customers relative to competition. Copy Catters are clear about the benefits they want to convey. However, their customers are hearing the same thing from their competitors. For example, every architecture and engineering firm is passionate about their work and showcases beautiful pictures of their projects. Every solar company touts the benefits of solar energy and shows example projects to back them up. Every pharmaceutical company cares about patients and uses cutting-edge technology to serve them.

Mind Trap Issues:
- Copy Catting strategy is to learn from what everyone else is doing and then attempt to do it a little bit better. Nothing is particularly unique or creative so there is no reason to select them relative to everyone else. Copy Catters will likely get their fair share of the market based on their outreach but are vulnerable to the competitor that ultimately

figures out how to break out from the pack. My goal is to help each business become that breakaway firm so they can gain a substantial market share.

- Copy Catters allow themselves to blend in, thinking, "This must be the right way of presenting my brand or business because that is what everyone else does. Those guys are smart, so this must be the way it is done in this category."

- It has not occurred to the Copy Catter that being relatively the same as everyone else provides little incentive for the prospect to work with them instead of their competitors.

- Communications end up being adequate, but not distinctive, as all the brands end up blending in a sea of monotony.

- Being stuck in Copy Catting mode commoditizes your brand and puts you in a position of needing to compete on price.

- Copy Catters say what they think they are supposed to say instead of what they really mean and why they uniquely matter in the world.

- Copy Catters will frequently have a meaningful disparity of how they view themselves and what they do internally relative to what they present to the world. The power of their true distinction ends up being underleveraged not only from a sales perspective, but also from a culture perspective. They end up missing out on claiming their true strengths.

Natural Habitats

Copy Catters typically live in financial services, wineries, pharma, healthcare, engineering, architecture, solar companies, printing companies, and grocery stores. The reality is we all have some of these tendencies because there is so much generic marketing and sales jargon that gets used across all categories that is familiar but is increasingly meaningless to customers. You might hear things like "We deliver excellent customer service," "your trusted partner," "providing excellent care," etc. It is very easy to have some Copy Catter tendencies without it being your primary Mind Trap.

KCL Case Study

Based in the heart of the Midwest, KCL is a mechanical and electrical engineering firm full of exceptional talent. Moreover, these self-proclaimed maverick engineers work together beautifully, love being around each other, and in their early days even opted to stay together in a smaller space when a second location was made available. Their positive culture and camaraderie allow for fruitful collaboration and they have a substantial list of really cool innovations. This group personifies the perfect balance of hard work and having fun.

The Before Picture

At a company level, KCL was a blatant Copy Catter. They looked outside their category at websites for inspiration, but ultimately made sure they checked the boxes of how to present themselves with comparisons to competitor websites. They fell into the standard engineering website that displays a rotating set of project pictures to convey experience and expertise along with language describing how smart, capable, and committed to clients they are.

The site was chock-full of typical "feel good" generic marketing speak that sounded good on the surface but, in reality did not convey anything a prospect would look at and think, "Wow!

Those guys are really doing something different over there and I need to work with them!"

Because the expectation of quality in the engineering category is so high, every firm knows how important it is to deliver to existing clients to avoid the need to replace them. Unfortunately for KCL, their company messaging was so unextraordinary, they only seemed to be able to acquire new projects in the rare instance when a new client was having a problem with their existing stable of engineers, which occurs only rarely.

When prompted with the concept of being a Copy Catter, KCL's leadership team immediately recognized the issue. This is one of the things that I love about the Mind Traps—it is easy for people to see the issue in themselves and then want to do something to correct it. Incrementally, the individuals responsible for account management and business development had their own Mind Traps—they were OverExplainers, Tacticians, and Day Jobbers. We set out to build a single powerful Rise Framework that would solve all the various Mind Traps to give them a powerful, centralizing way of conveying themselves that would break them out of the pack and give prospect distinctive reasons to work with them instead of a competitor.

Overall, the before picture was a company that presented itself showing a portfolio of projects they were passionate about with clients who loved working with them. They were having difficulty winning new clients because they sounded like every other firm.

The After Picture with the Rise Framework

We completed a series of interviews with the client's leadership team and with some of their customers. We looked for underleveraged assets and unsatisfied needs in the category. We then completed our Rise Workshop, which involves getting the leadership team together for the better part of one day.

The first question I always ask is, "If you were to encounter a prospect who knew nothing of your offering and you could tell them up to three reasons why they should buy your solution instead of somebody else's, what would you say?" This question tells me a lot about how leadership views themselves and reveals what their Mind Traps are. One of two things consistently happens. I either get a shorter, focused list of reasons that are not unique relative to competition, or I get a long list of widely varying reasons. Regardless of which one it is, it is the perfect tee-up for why we need to build the Rise Framework.

When there is a wide disparity in language being used across your organization, you don't have a brand, you have a collection of ideas that do not add up to a powerful distinctive Promise or conclusion of why you matter. This is the noise your prospects are hearing in the world, which erodes rather than strengthens conversion rates and leaves you vulnerable to competitors who develop a clear and powerful value proposition. When we did this exercise with KCL, it was clear they had many awesome qualities they saw in themselves and the reasons for a client to choose their firm—but they did not know how to best articulate these so they blended in with everyone else.

The available underserved needs in the mechanical engineering world are more limited than most categories because the quality-of-service bar is so high. In talking with their clients, we found that the standard required for competitive advantage was going to be higher than any category I'd ever encountered. Getting exceptional work, having a great portfolio of projects to tout, and being super responsive were all expected. These were also the exact same talking points every competitor in the space emphasized, making these qualities merely table stakes.

It was apparent none of these traits would ever work to win new clients unless our client happened to hit a prospect at a time when one of their stable of providers had screwed up, which almost never happened. I had to dig harder for white space market opportunities and found some. . . they are always there. In this case, there was room to address two major unmet needs that could be developed into a competitive advantage. The one good thing about being in a Copy Catter category is that all the competitors are saying the same thing: if a Copy Catter can shift to convey valuable distinctive qualities, they can seriously stand out.

We landed on the following key elements in KCL Rise Framework and I will share how we came there. I always look to build the Proof Points and Pillars first and then look for the gestalt of the Pillars that all adds up to the Promise. I also always look for a healthy blend of what the company is doing today, but also what it could naturally become based on its inherent strengths. In this way the Framework has strong inherent qualities with room to grow and continue to evolve down a path to success.

Helping to Build the World we All Want to Live In

| The Perfect Extension to Your Team | Relentless Attention to Detail | Practical, Inspired Innovation |

Pillar 1: *Be the Perfect Extension of Your Team.* KCL's clients are generally architects. While responsiveness and client service are generic marketing speak, setting the bar higher to be the perfect extension of the architect or client team is new and distinctive. This would require some very doable improvements to the current process to act as verifiable Proof Points. Much of what was required, they were doing anyway. But enhancements could move the bar higher to a place of meaningful distinction, and by being more intentional in the process they could be superior to competitors and have a stronger story to tell.

Being the Perfect Extension of The Client's Team Pillar means:

- Starting with the deepest respect for our client relationships. We appreciate how valuable every client relationship is and we view ourselves as having an important role in strengthening that even further.

- Developing an engagement framework/form we complete with clients to interact perfectly with how the architect would like to engage—done at an individual project manager level and covering the important elements of where, when, and how we would like to communicate.

- Hiring and training our people to speak Engineer, Architect, and Human. We want to feel proud of the people we put in front of our clients as an extension of the best of who we are. As a note here: a lot of engineering firms struggle with this as engineers tend to be either introverted or overly technical and long-winded, or both. There is a joke in the engineering world . . . What is the difference between an introverted and extroverted engineer? The answer: The extroverted engineer stares at your shoes instead of their own! We intentionally hire and train individuals to be good in front of clients and to operate in the third person instead of the first person. This means we take responsibility for the conclusions we are creating among the audience and not just rattling off what might be interesting to us.

- Project Wrap Up. We focus on Client Delight versus Satisfaction. At the end of each project, we are going to ask you to complete a three-minute survey to see how we did. We share whatever you are comfortable sharing with our entire team which inspires us all to perform. We grow through referrals and invite you to share your experiences with us with others.

Notice how different the communication is above relative to saying the standard category of rhetoric: "We provide great client service." It's massive, and has proven to completely change the nature of the conversation with prospects who take what KCL is saying seriously because it is new and full of depth.

Pillar 2: *Relentless Attention to Detail.* This Pillar emerged in the other white space we identified around problem prevention and resolution. The challenge for building projects is that profitability can be won or lost based on problems that emerge in the field. It is not that engineering companies are bad at this; they are pretty good, actually. But since this is such an important part of success where risk and reward are so great, there was an opportunity to set the bar even higher.

The Pillar became *Relentless Attention to Detail,* which is a more powerful way of conveying another overused generic term, "quality control." We then developed the Proof Points and Power Plant to validate this Pillar (there are two major ways problems kill projects and we focus on both). This encompassed the following:

- Our *Preemptive Problem Detection Process* prevents problems from occurring. Proof Points include: 1) use of the most advanced 3D visioning capabilities; 2) formal partner review where the general contractors and subcontractors convene to consider where potential conflicts could arise with particular attention to where systems overlap; 3) superior sequencing in the field which saves time and money where equipment or infrastructure can be shared; 4) our teams jointly signing off, which enhances collaboration and teamwork while reducing the risk of finger pointing.

- As good as that is, no one is perfect, so we built our own *Problem Resolution Process.* Proof Points: 1) quick, course-correction approach to minimize costs and disruption. We built this approach in a more intentional way that elevates problem detection immediately to the team lead who is always on call; 2) training to be client-first in these situations with immediate remedy steps succinctly highlighted and directed to get the project on track; 3) taking a collaborative leadership approach with other teams on the project, constantly vigilant to potential risks from any source; 4) acting like we own it—doing what we would do if we were the property owner.

Pillar 3: *Practical, Inspired Innovation.* The biggest underleveraged asset for KCL was their strength of innovation. During the workshop, it became evident they had done some amazing technical innovations. They even created their own construction company to handle some of their innovations because the existing market of contractors did not have the skills to execute some of these projects. As a result, they found it easier to build their own contracting company they kept separate to avoid a client feeling threatened by the possible risk that an in-house contractor might attempt to steal work from them.

One innovation example was their complete solution for a cold storage facility to thaw the frozen ground under the building that started to cause problems for the building. They used the heat produced from the refrigeration units to keep the ground at the proper temperature with a high degree of precision to save energy. The systems they developed could have benefits for many cold storage facilities. They also had impressive geothermal systems and specialty lighting capabilities they had developed.

The company buried these innovations for fear that any of them might pigeonhole the company into smaller, less frequent specialty projects. They were also worried these innovations might require the development of costly sister companies to house the innovation to avoid these risks. We rewired the thinking around this entire topic, turning the innovations into assets. With a stronger overarching brand structure, these innovations could be used to support and strengthen an overall conclusion rather than compete with or overpower it.

Moreover, by making *Practical, Inspired Innovation* into one of the core Pillars of strength for the company and each individual innovation a Proof Point rather than a headline, we would be contributing to a much stronger brand position for the company that could broaden their breadth of client services considerably. This concept worked beautifully . . . it also started to create a space that was more aligned with their internally recognized maverick qualities that helped attract talent as new hires were encouraged to nurture their own innovations!

In effect, what we did with KCL was to dial up three processes that were underleveraged. We just had to convey them distinctively and elevate them internally so they would be powerful and unique relative to competitors, giving sales, marketing, and project teams the means to stand out in this competitive environment.

The Promise

With these Pillars combined, the Promise for KCL became "Helping to Build the World We All Want to Live In." There are several things I love about this Promise. Let's consider the words . . .

- The Promise is both bold and humble at the same time. We help, but we are not alone in impacting the world. It invites others to join in the dream.
- It allows human excellence and connection to coexist.
- It invites a question . . . what do you mean by that, or how do you do that? Both lead to a more natural means of explaining the business.
- It also conveys that there is innovation involved . . . but that the innovation is for a better, more fulfilling life. People would like to see a better world today and would like to join with companies who are inspired to help provide that.
- It is a Promise that attracts talented people who are drawn to the service of something greater than themselves.

And most importantly, it is True, Meaningful, and Distinct for the KCL brand and business . . . its origins, its purpose, its future. They could prove it immediately, with room for continued growth and development over time.

KCL's complete Rise Framework . . .

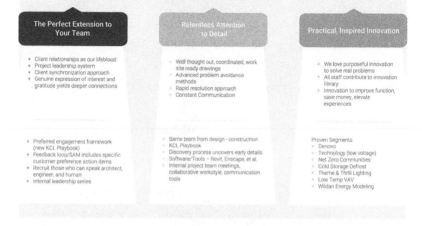

The important thing about developing your Rise Framework is to build on inherent strengths and tendencies so when the company chooses to focus on them, they will be able to comfortably execute with room for improvement. It is already true in their way of being, but now will be done in a way that can be presented more distinctively to win more business.

Target Impact

With the Rise Framework defined, the first step was to circle back on KCL's closest prospects—additional partners within firms where they already had existing but underdeveloped relationships—with a new, more compelling story to be told to get them over the finish line.

Next, we focused on client relationships that had national footprints. Senior housing came first and it became the first service area that broke them out of their local market.

Lastly, we focused on the underleveraged innovations that had been developed, but not yet materialized into business prospecting. We pursued the ones with the greatest benefits to the greatest number of prospects.

Most importantly, KCL increased sales, immediately winning a new $500,000 project and sales lift of over 40 percent. Now whenever I talk to anyone at KCL, they tell me how their framework has helped them rise above competitors to get new contracts. It is extremely gratifying to see them Claim the Top of Their Mountain.

Culture Shift

So often, culture and values are described in a generic idealized code of conduct that looks good on paper but is beyond the bounds of human nature. We like to build culture around the distinctive qualities that align with the evolved business proposition. Culture follows the naturally occurring pride of being exceptional with clarity about why you matter in the world to those you serve. These are the qualities that help people feel unified in a mission that is greater than themselves and those are the environments where thriving cultures are found.

The company already had a great culture of camaraderie. Under this framework, KCL was able to:

- Elevate and unify the pride in working there. The team now takes ownership of describing where they work with an enhanced sense of being part of something bigger than themselves. The values and distinctions of the company are reinforced regularly in company meetings and signage is present on-site reinforcing their approach to business.

- Encourage innovation around practically inspired applications. Each person and innovation is valued and could become a development territory for new business segments managed by the innovator. This also becomes a quality that helps to attract the type of talent they seek.

- Use the Rise Framework in personnel reviews assessing support for the overall Promise, support of innovation, client enthusiasm, and number of reported client problems.

This is a great example of how a single, powerful framework effectively drives sales, marketing, targeting, operations, and culture. Bravo, KCL!

Comments from KCL's Kris Kunze and James Deeds, Managing Principals and Julie Eliason, CMO

"We came to know Doug through Victoria Sassine, with whom we have had a long-term relationship where she ran the Goldman Sachs 10,000 Entrepreneur Program. As soon as Doug told us we were Copy Catters, we knew he was right. What was funny was that we had convinced ourselves we were not because we had gathered inspiration from outside the category as well, but at the end of the day we looked and sounded like everyone else."

"Working with Doug has been transformative to our business. With the new positioning, we immediately used it to help land a $500,000 contract. Our close rate has moved up substantially and we are winning the projects and clients we want. We have also been able to edge up our pricing which immediately elevates earnings. We spent the time to clearly define how we are the perfect partner for our clients and they gravitate to it strongly and the attention to detail bolstered our quality processes."

"The clarity of how and why we matter in the world makes life so much easier for us. We know exactly what to say and how to say it, which has fed everyone throughout our company. Doug and Victoria helped us refine our targeting and innovation approach so we are much clearer and on target with respect to how we should be focusing our time. I didn't know things could be this good!"

CHAPTER NINE

THE OVEREXPLAINER

F alling into the **OverExplainer** Mind Trap happens when someone lacks a clear, concise purpose for being. OverExplainers add more and more content or descriptions that come to the sellers' minds during the pitch with the hope that one of them will stick. Much like a meandering river, this is the common description I hear from OverExplainers in describing their sales strategy: "I keep talking until I find the point where my prospect's eyes light up, and then I focus there." What they do not realize is often the prospect's eyes lit up the moment they figured out the excuse to get out of the conversation because too much of their time was being taken up without sufficient benefit or purpose.

Mind Trap Issues:

- Buyers want clarity in purpose and expect brands and salespeople to articulate it. In effect, many prospects inherently feel that if you cannot efficiently tell them what you do and why you matter in the world, you can't expect them to invest the effort to figure it out on your behalf! They have lived without your product this long, and chances are they will be fine without it going forward.

- In the Information Age, attention spans are getting shorter and shorter, and the challenge for the OverExplainer grows greater and greater.
- OverExplainers can unintentionally raise risk elements the buyer has not been thinking about.
- When in OverExplainer mode, you don't realize that every point made has an exponential impact on the number of mental calculations a prospect has to consider. As explained earlier, buyers don't consider each point in isolation. All the information has to logically coexist.

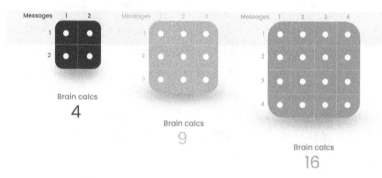

Natural Habitats

OverExplaining is commonly found in education and non-profits. It also tends to emerge with passionate entrepreneurs. The OverExplainer tendency is more of a personality driven than professionally driven Mind Trap. These are individuals who have always tended toward being more talkative, operating from a more free-flowing way of speaking that is less organized and structured. For them all of these details matter and they struggle to prioritize and organize them from the lens of how the prospect would best absorb them.

La Jolla Country Day School Case Study

We had just moved and settled our family into a new home in La Jolla. It was a typical gorgeous day in Southern California when I took our very excited, covertly apprehensive daughter to her first day at La Jolla Country Day School. We obviously put a lot of thought into where we wanted our daughter to be educated, but at this point in time, Country Day was an educational underdog. The school had a bit of an inferiority complex relative to its chief rival in town, which had a reputation of being the more elite Ivy League feeder school. However, the competitor school was also viewed as being less considerate to its students. They had a reputation to uphold, and parents and students needed to recognize this and comply with the standards.

The Before Picture

Parents who chose Country Day wanted an environment that was a bit kinder and gentler. But in general, parents who chose Country Day felt a twinge of angst at sending their child to the "second-tier school" in the area. When I dropped off our sweet girl, I gave her a hug just long enough to provide her with comfort and just short enough to avoid embarrassment (it's a tough balance), and I proudly watched her walk into her classroom. On the way out, as luck would have it, I ran into the headmaster. He asked about my occupation, and then my 30-second response turned into an hour-long conversation. Three weeks later I was running our Rise workshop for the school board and school leadership.

The After Picture with the Rise Framework

We began the workshop with Country Day like we do with the senior leadership of every company we work with. First, we asked each participant to pretend they are speaking to a prospect about their offering who knows little to nothing about the school: "If the prospect were to ask for up to the three reasons why they should consider your proposition relative to a competitive alternative, what would you say?"

We have everyone in the room write these items down so they do not bias each other. Then we go around the room and have each person tell what they wrote as we scribe the answers for the room to see. This exercise yields a laundry list of what their team collectively conveys to the world. The answers were expected . . . our teachers are very good here, your child gets a more personalized education, it's a very strong community, we have very good facilities, etc. The list went on and on, but nothing distinguished them. Every benefit they listed was nearly identical to what every other private school would say.

Knowing schools often exhibit OverExplainer and Copy Catter Mind Traps, during this workshop, I put up the school's very lengthy mission statement on the screen, then added the very lengthy mission statements for Country Day's two key competitors. The degree of overlap of these three mission statements was enormous, further hammering home the lack of distinction and the overuse of nice-sounding generic marketing speak. It was overwhelming and Country Day's admission rate was being directly affected by its OverExplainer Mind Trap.

In essence, La Jolla Country Day was conveying the same lengthy story of all private schools with the added barrier of having a bit of an inferiority complex.

Deliberately searching to find what sets your organization apart is paramount to remedy the OverExplainer Mind Trap. During the Country Day workshop, one of the key distinctions that emerged was introduced by the Headmaster. He made an effort to actively engage with noneducation global leaders to bring a richer, more complete worldview to education. From other work I had done in education, I knew that the single biggest problem kids have with school today is lack of relevance . . . as in, "What is the point of learning this?" "When will I ever use this in real life?"

Amazingly enough, this is the same issue with school we had when we were kids, because in many ways education has not changed much over the years. La Jolla Country Day School's focus on this greater connection to the real world would be the critical nugget we would build upon.

The Promise we landed on was "Inspiring Greatness for a Better World," which is messaging you never hear a school try to convey. What became more powerful was the underlying storyline we crafted. It turns out there are four factors predictive in identifying people who attain greatness in the world as defined by making great contributions to society, not necessarily financial gain. Two of the predictors are about the nature of the people themselves and two are about the environments they grew up in.

The Two People Factors:
- People who attain greatness are hard workers.
- They are also people of character whom mentors wanted to support.

The Two Environmental Factors:
- They grew up with access to resources and mentors not available in other places.
- Those places they grew up in had a "what if" mindset instead of a "that is" mentality. In other words, they valued exploration of possibilities over proving pre-set conclusions.

Put together, we landed on the following simple, yet distinctively powerful value proposition . . .

> *Bring your child of character who is willing to work hard, and we will provide access to resources and mentors not commonly found in other places in a "what if" environment that surrounds your child with the greatest opportunity to achieve greatness.*

That shift in storyline was huge for the school. It was wonderful how the entire community embraced and was unified around this new language. Educators created videos of how they went about inspiring greatness for a better world in their classrooms. The admissions team used this messaging to tell the story. Tours of the school increasingly became about conveying this conclusion versus just showing the family around the school. The entire community came onboard.

**Inspiring Greatness
for a Better World**

Hard Work & Character Coming Together	World View of Academics and Beyond	Fulfilling Your Child's Potential

Country Day already had a more student-friendly approach. This was the reason we chose the school for our daughter over the top competitor in the area. We were looking for a high level of education, without an ulcer-inducing culture. Now that Country Day unapologetically emphasized this characteristic of the school, it became clear that this new approach was truly an unmet need in the market and that many parents in the community wanted this same type of educational experience for their children.

One of the great benefits of starting with the branding approach is it provides the framework for telling the story of what you are doing in a more compelling way. One of the other important benefits is that it provides a construct for future enhancements or innovations for any business, including a school. At Country Day, the administration receives constant input from parents and educators and other stakeholders at a rate of about five new ideas each week. In the past, these ideas were all treated as a bunch of one-offs and it was hard to evaluate which ideas to pursue and which to table.

Before, each concept was appraised on its own merits. As a result, many ideas that were pursued might have had individual benefits but did little to elevate the overall conclusion about the institution. Today, new ideas are evaluated against their ability to fit within the overall Rise Framework, within one or more Pillars, and provide a clear line of sight to supporting the overall Brand Promise of "Inspiring Greatness for a Better World." This provides a lasting competitive advantage that continues to lift the school.

Country Day, like many of my clients, feels that their Rise Framework is a part of their strategic advantage and asked that I not share the more granular details of their framework in this book.

Target Impact

Country Day's Brand Promise and core value of dignity has become the north star for the school community. As a result of Country Day's clear Promise, value proposition, and more focused targeting approach, applications increased by over 100 percent. Giving to the school has also increased by over 100 percent. These changes have impacted the lives of thousands of children who learn at an institution that is preparing them for a world where they expect to contribute and succeed.

Culture Shift

The part of this case I love the most is that the people involved with the school shifted their mindsets. They went from feeling like underdogs to being unified around a higher purpose with greater lasting impact on helping their students find greatness. Part of what we did during this process was to give an eloquent voice to the underlying motivation of parents who chose Country Day over their rival. The Promise was powerful, and definitely set the school apart. At the rival school, the child was there to serve the glory of the school, but at Country Day, the school was there for the glory of the student.

It has been amazing to watch as Country Day continues to teach and mentor and help its students see new possibilities. And guess what? They also get those kids into great colleges. Admissions at Country Day went up while admissions at the cross-town rivals went down. Being more than a bit competitive myself, I must say I delighted in all of that. I give Headmaster Dr. Gary Krahn a great deal of credit for having the courage to invite me to lead this process and then to embrace the advice we offered.

Comments From Dr. Gary Krahn, Headmaster of La Jolla Country Day School

"La Jolla Country Day school has always been a great school with impactful teachers and a mission to intellectual exploration, personal growth, and social responsibility. We were missing an understanding of what made us remarkable and how to share this with our community.

"As the Head of School with 35 years of experience, I know how to lead a school. Doug helped us coordinate and unleash the full potential of our school. Doug Harrison has an uncanny ability to listen and to form innovative connections between ideas. As we reflect back upon his work, Doug facilitated conversations to allow us to see things that would have remained invisible. Doug uncovered the heart and soul of our school and then developed the language to market our unique school families. Doug moved us from a collection of educational abstractions to our overarching Promise to our community. He earned our respect. We value his expertise and we are grateful for his unwavering commitment to our success."

CHAPTER 10

THE PILLAR PITCHER

———— ▬ ————

Those in the **Pillar Pitcher** Mind Trap are thoughtful about their value proposition, having done the work of recognizing three or four underlying Pillars that support the value proposition. This is actually the most advanced of the 10 Mind Traps, as this sales and marketing approach is doing many of the right things. Chances are the sales and marketing teams have built out materials and messaging that convey these benefits, and they work. At the same time, I have never met an individual or company that is doing everything at fully optimized levels, so the opportunity is to take what you are doing well and do it even better.

Mind Trap Issues:
- Pillars are presented predominantly from the seller's point of view. "This is what you need to know about what I have to offer you."
- The time spent envisioning and empathizing with the conclusions prospects draw based on the sum of every-

thing they can learn about your offering from any source is minimal.

- Pillar Pitchers have one way of telling their story regardless of the circumstances, making it harder to adjust to the time made available by the prospect.
- Consider the three shiny apples parable: the three shiny apples represent the three Pillars of the value proposition that the seller emphasizes in their pitch. What is overlooked is that the buyer is examining the *entire basket of apples*, not just the three shiny ones, looking for any bad or questionable apples from any source.
- If a buyer can find one bad apple (any negative details they might discover online, in a showroom, from other points being made, on a package, how you look or speak, etc.), then they have reason to reject the entire proposition because risk is present. One negative risk element can outweigh 10 positive ones because buyers seek to manage risk first.
- The reward when a prospect finds a blemish in the basket of apples is that it justifies rejection which allows them to keep their money in their pocket and feel like a smart shopper.
- Sellers assume everyone should want to buy their products. The reality is prospects are looking for reasons not to buy. Sellers sell benefits, while buyers are inherently looking to avoid risk.

Natural Habitats

Pillar Pitchers are present across all categories where there is a greater dependence on marketing. Organizations that struggle with the Pillar Pitcher Mind Trap view sales and marketing as an important part of the organization and invest heavily in these areas.

Rombauer Case Study

When Koerner Rombauer settled on a hilltop property in Napa Valley, he was a commercial airline pilot who spent his free time learning about wine. But after less than a decade, he and his wife founded Rombauer Vineyards and produced wines, especially their Chardonnay, that are beloved around the world and dominate the over-$25 segment. They have a great assortment of wine varietals with a steady growth history. Even more wonderfully, they have an outstanding and dedicated team committed to going the extra mile to do things right top to bottom. Koerner Rombauer was a pioneer winemaker in Napa and almost every staff member has their own memory or favorite story that illustrates Koerner's larger-than-life personality.

The Before Picture

Sadly, a couple of years ago, Koerner passed away, and his passing took some of the natural emotion inherent in the brand with it. The new leadership team stepped in and worked hard to do all the right things to continue to grow the brand, add varietals, improve quality, and nurture the staff. And, while the business continued to grow and prosper, it felt like something was missing. The emotional expression of the brand and its presentation to the world had become more limited. The character of Koerner Rombauer had been the lifeblood behind the business, but it was no longer present to carry the more emotionally meaningful qualities of the brand and sales message forward.

In conveying the Rombauer brand to the world, the company relied on pitching their three main Pillars. They were proud of their heritage as a family-owned business, would describe category leadership in the $25+ Chardonnay segment, and showed a strong portfolio of great quality wines. It was not that anything was wrong in a financial sense, because the brand was continuing to grow, but there was an emotional resonance to inspire purchasing and company culture that was missing, leaving the brand and business vulnerable to future erosion. For me, upon entering our workshop process I was determined to find the emotional resonance of the brand—and we did, big time!

The After Picture with the Rise Framework

One of the things I noticed early on was that each bottle of Rombauer wine has a cork with the words "The Joy of Wine" printed upon it. This is a nod to Rombauer's Aunt Irma, who wrote *The Joy of Cooking* in 1931. Her book is one of the top-selling cookbooks of all time, having sold more than 18 million copies worldwide. The Becker family, who are descendants of the Irma Rombauer family, continue to periodically update and refresh the cookbook with new editions. Other than noting this interesting relationship, some suggested food pairings, and copies of the cookbook for sale in the tasting rooms, Rombauer Vineyards did relatively little with possible connections to the emotional outcome of joy.

I was intrigued with the idea of leveraging Joy, or the Joy of Wine, more with Rombauer and asked if they had considered that possibility. I learned that the wine and cookbook sides of the family were only loosely connected in the present day and that the future of cookbooks in the world of internet recipes felt like a risk that could potentially erode this connection to Joy. In effect, the vineyard leadership team had discounted or eliminated any significant use of Joy because they associated that asset with the cookbook side of the family operations, an area where they did not have control.

During our business-building process, everything was going well, but I was still not finding much emotion from the team. Everyone was great and doing their part, but there was not a lot of inspiration happening. It was at that point that I asked each person to write down their favorite Koerner story. It was that exercise that revealed the true Joy of Wine, relationships with wine, and relationships with Koerner Rombauer himself that each employee felt grateful to have experienced in their lives.

After sharing these stories, it was like a fog in the room had lifted and the celebration of Koerner's life and legacy and the joy that is Rombauer wines could emerge. They had more than enough joy in their own wine brand and their own experiences to own "Joyful Moments" and the Joy of Wine—and no other wine brand owned that space.

Since the Brand Promise became about owning the Joy of Wine and Joyful Moments, we nurtured two emotional connections to be made around Rombauer wine drinking occasions. Every time a person opens a bottle of Rombauer and shares it with a friend or family member, we want them to embrace the joyful moment or memory they are about to make. And every time they are having a joyful moment in their lives, big or small, we want that to trigger the thought that this might also be a good time to have a glass of Rombauer wine. To be part of the joyful moments of the lives of those you serve is a very wonderful thing indeed, and a wonderful gift for the world!

The Joy Of Wine

Koerner's Values | A Wine for the People | Joyful Moments

Promise: The Joy of Wine

Pillar 1: Koerner's Values. We replaced "Heritage" and "Family Owned" with Koerner's Values as the first Pillar. Why? Heritage and family owned would make Rombauer sound like too many other brands. It is uninteresting and uninspiring. The point is Koerner's Values are alive and well today. Koerner went from pilot to Napa Valley pioneer and was red, white, and blue through and through. He was a passionate brand evangelist who nurtured a devoted following with charisma that continues to inspire the company culture today. Members of the team could then personalize the description with their own Koerner connection.

Pillar 2: A Wine for the People. The second became A Wine for the People, which is at the same time exclusive yet accessible and very drinkable. The original "House of Fine Wines" Pillar would again put Rombauer on everyone else's playing field when they could own their own. *A Wine for the People* enables a better story of how the portfolio emerged from the passion developed around Rombauer drinkers with a loyalty that is unmatched. Rombauer didn't expand to make money so much as to serve their drinkers.

The Pillar of A Wine for the People also emerged around the insight that sommeliers at certain restaurants would not take on Rombauer wine because for some of them it was considered too popular. The insight we brought to counter that objection is how Rombauer buyers love their wine. There are lots of them, and they are less interested in experimenting with a wine they might be disappointed in than having their tried-and-true favorite. That is why you want Rombauer wines at your restaurant.

Pillar 3: Joyful Moments. Joyful Moments became the relational quality we wanted to inspire because it is more active and ongoing to drive more frequent consumption than Joyful Memories, which was also being considered. It includes elements that happiness is a choice well-made and repeated and that joyful moments together become cherished memories anchored in gratitude. All this keeps Koerner's spirit alive and well, which brings us full circle to the first Pillar of Koerner's values.

There are two primary things I want to emphasize about this new construct. The first is we built a unique playing field uniquely expressed by Rombauer in a very cluttered wine market. The second is that both the Promise and each Pillar invite questions from the prospect . . . "What do you mean by Koerner's Values? What do you mean by a Wine for the People? What do you mean about owning Joyful Moments?" We are no longer "selling;" we are instead inviting the listener to become part of our story and to become inspired to join a magnificent brand and product experience.

Marketing Impact

The Promise provides a centralizing and clarifying framework for all communications. Without Joy and Joyful Moments as the centralizing point of the spear, every ad, promotion, and communication was treated as a one-off. In other words, the marketing team would be in a position of wondering what sort of things they should say in the Sauvignon Blanc messaging and would look for different things than what they might say for another varietal or promotion in an attempt to be interesting. This would actually diffuse rather than strengthen a singular conclusion they would hope to inspire and add time to each initiative.

With Joy at the helm, now every message or outreach becomes the question: "How do we want to present Joy or Joyful Moments this time?" It becomes a question of how to stay on brand and reinforce this wonderful conclusion we want our drinkers to have about us over time. For copywriters and promotion creators, this can be half the battle. And for drinkers, the reward is also wonderful because the reinforcement of a joyful experience received is also delicious. It is a diversity of experiences joined in a single conclusion.

Culture Shift

The decision to unify company culture under the concept of Joyful Moments also enhanced customer experiences. This might be most apparent in the tasting room where the company has continued to elevate the nature of engagement with guests. It aligns the team around a common outcome that places greater emphasis on experiencing joyful moments together above the basic descriptions encountered during more typical tasting room encounters. Joyfulness is increasingly woven into the fabric of supporting materials and language.

The company also created a *Joy of Wine* video, to which many of the team members contributed. This, along with the entire brand framework, is used in the onboarding of new employees to tell the story of Rombauer wines and how each employee is considered an ambassador for Joy in and outside of the office.

With the Promise, each member of the team has an easier time describing what they contribute to the lives of those they serve, and it elevates the spirit of the team around something that is bigger than themselves. It supports their history with Rombauer and their future, living his legacy.

Today, Rombauer continues to grow and flourish at unprecedented levels and I still have a massive bottle of Rombauer Chardonnay signed by the entire team that sits proudly in my dining room as a reminder of the Joy we created together.

Comments From Robert Knebel, CEO, Rombauer Vineyards

"I've asked Doug to help me on engagements with three different companies over the past 12 years. His decades of research and consulting work with many of the most famous brands in the world have provided deep and relevant insights into human behavior and business cultures. Doug is exceptionally effective in engaging every session participant in meaningful dialog. In a short period of time, with careful listening, he simply gets to the heart of people's feelings on any subject, and he does it in a manner that makes people feel safe to share their thoughts.

"He synthesizes participants' own comments into summary position statements that leave everyone with a sense of deep satisfaction that they now know who they are, what matters most, how to express that, and with clear direction on 'next steps.' An engagement with Doug makes a permanent and very positive impact on your business and on a personal level with every participant.

"For Rombauer Vineyards specifically, we love building around the concept of Joy. It is a perfect fit for who and what we are and has focused the emotional energy of our brand into the truth of why our customers are drawn to us. We use the framework on events and marketing and in our training and onboarding. Every employee is an ambassador for Joy in the world and we want everyone on our team to feel unified in contributing to making the world a happier place to be."

CHAPTER ELEVEN
THE FEATURE LISTER

Those in **Feature Lister** mode have the good fortune of having a feature-rich offering. Often, but not always, there is a heavy focus on product specifications in the development process or the offering may have earned awards or accolades from industry groups that the seller wants to highlight. The natural attention to these specifications turns a product presentation into a feature list. The logical intent behind the Mind Trap is to present an overwhelming case of good reasons to buy.

Mind Trap Issues:
- When you Feature List, the greater vision of how the product changes your customer's life (the before and after picture of the core problem being solved for them) gets lost and with that loss, so goes the opportunity to create the emotional impact that is the ultimate motivation for purchase.
- Buyers want to feel the vision of how their life will be better with your product in it. An overemphasis on feature lists erodes the opportunity to create that emotional connection.

- Great sales presentations have an equal balance of overall brand meaning, critical product features, and a meaningful salesperson's story.
- The irony when Feature Listing is that it actually makes you more like a commodity as you become an overwhelming list of stuff that has lost its opportunity to have greater emotional resonance.
- Being in Feature Lister mode hurts margins, because when the list of features alone is insufficient to inspire conversion, Feature Listers will often then turn to price reductions. Their reasoning is, "I told them everything we have, and they still did not buy. It must be that our price is too high." They are completely unaware that the issue was failure to inspire a vision of an improved life.
- Feature Listers do not realize that every point they make has an exponential impact on the number of mental calculations a prospect must consider . . . in other words, buyers don't consider each point in isolation. In their effort to avoid risk, prospects consider each point you make in combination with every other point to assess if they can all logically coexist.

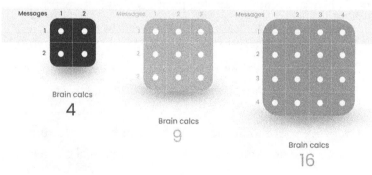

Natural Habitats

Feature Listers are often, but not exclusively, found in tech companies, private aviation, biotech, natural supplements, or in other categories with more complex propositions.

Many salespeople love to go into Feature Lister mode. Their sales mindset is, "If I can convince a customer to hear my pitch of product features and if they don't buy, it is the product's fault or price because I told them all about it." In reality, it's the failure to convey a vision of how the customer's life will be improved by the offering. Salespeople will find their lives are much happier when they do more to bring the brand vision and their love of what they do earlier in the discussion.

Banatrol Plus Case Study

I love the team over at Medtrition, which is a medical food company and the makers of Banatrol Plus. They are all about helping people and they have found a way to do this by offering specially formulated, natural medical foods designed to nourish the body, speed recovery, and reduce costs for people suffering from health conditions. While this company is pretty solid on what they do and why they matter to the world, I want to show you how the Rise Framework process applies to lower involvement categories like packaged goods.

The Before Picture

When we met them, this was Medtrition's direct-to-consumer marketing for their product Banatrol Plus, which is the largest natural anti-diarrhea product sold today. There are so many details, the important assets of the product offering are lost. The imagery behind it makes it even more challenging on the eye and the overemphasis on the bananas makes it seems like it might just be banana flakes, which is not going to build efficacy expectations.

The product has a prebiotic which for most people is unknown. Probiotics pass through your system with each dosage so you always need to be taking them. Prebiotics help eliminate bad bacteria in your digestive tract and set up new colonies of good bacteria for better ongoing health. The ad below is a clear example of a Feature Lister approach to selling, and it is overwhelming!

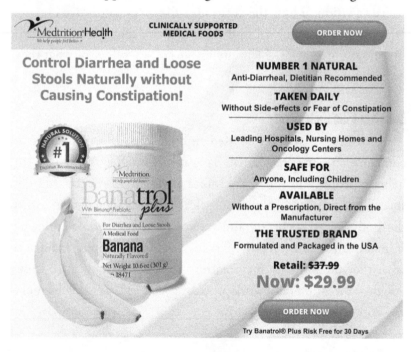

The After Picture with the Rise Framework

For the new sales approach, we wanted to make sure people really understood why Banatrol Plus was such an innovative product. One of the things I have learned about natural products, after working with dozens of them, is that there is an inherent belief that they are not going to work as well as their conventional counterparts. Buyers are trading off a natural remedy for one that actually works well. This would certainly be assumed for Banatrol Plus since the ad prominently features pictures of bananas. We landed on the following Promise and Pillars for Banatrol Plus.

Win the War Against Diarrhea

My Body, My Solution

Sustainable Diarrhea Control

Take My Personal Power Back

Diarrhea sufferers, especially those with chronic conditions like IBS-D, need help with their daily digestion. In talking with chronic sufferers who are the ideal target for this product, their digestive system feels like a war zone, which was the insight that helped lead to the Promise. Leading diarrhea products like Imodium, while temporarily effective, actually work against your body by shutting down your digestion. For chronic sufferers, using conventional products leads them to this ongoing misery of turning their digestion on and off, which is never going to be a good thing. The fact that Banatrol Plus can be used daily and supports the digestive system is a huge asset that fills an unmet need in the market.

We set out to support an ad campaign that followed the Rise Framework. We worked with Medtrition to create a new sales approach designed to accomplish the following:

- Use a description that recognizes that this is a war for those who are suffering chronic diarrhea, whose body can feel like they are in a war zone.
- Craft a new message charged with power and action, which are needed to battle such a formidable adversary. This energy matches the battle happening in the lives of sufferers.
- Simplify the storyline and break free of the Feature Lister Mind Trap. The historical approach was overwhelming and confusing for a prospective customer.
- Use language that implies use for chronic diarrhea without explicitly alienating those who might need to use the product occasionally instead of daily.
- Efficiently convey how we help equip a sufferer's body army to fight back and win using simple descriptions that are more clear, distinct, and powerful.
- More assertively, and simply, distinguish prebiotic versus probiotic.
- Circle back on competitors with another familiar analogy of stop-and-go traffic to convey they are not a good solution and actually hurt sufferers.
- Lock in a validation point of efficacy with the #1 product.

With the Rise Framework in place, the new messaging storyline became:

Win the War against Diarrhea

Diarrhea can make your gut feel like a battle zone. Banatrol Plus powers your gut to fight back and win naturally!

- *Bimuno PREbiotic builds your army of good bacteria to digest food while depleting the bad bacteria.*
- *A proprietary blend of banana flakes absorbs water and solidifies your stool.*
- *Other over-the-counter medications may temporarily win the battle but lose the war!*
- *Conventional diarrhea products shut your gut down temporarily. It's like being in stop and go traffic and it's awful for your body!*
- *PRObiotics just pass through and do not build your army of good bacteria essential to good ongoing gut health.*

  Banatrol Plus is the medical food that keeps your body winning the war against diarrhea. See why we are the #1 natural anti-diarrhea product used and recommended by medical professionals.

Target Impact

Another part of this project we included was updating the targeting approach for Banatrol Plus. Their ongoing direct-to-consumer approach relied on Facebook ads using lookalike targeting tactics. For those of you not familiar with lookalike targeting, the marketer puts their proposition out into the world and obtains a base of customers. They then select an option where Facebook uses an algorithm to go find more of them and show them this ad. It can be a wonderful tool.

In this case, the tool was not serving them well. In looking into the sales data, we found that repeat rates and frequency of purchasing were low and were occurring primarily among older women. The reality was Banatrol Plus was not being purchased, for the most part, by chronic sufferers. Instead, it was being purchased mostly by episodic sufferers. This is the downside of lookalike marketing, because if you go fishing in the wrong pond, you are going to just keep fishing there, not realizing that there is this much bigger pond not far away that has bigger fish to catch.

After Medtrition adopted this new messaging, targeting ad sales, repeat rates, and the average lifetime value of customers have increased by double digits and are continuing to grow.

Culture Shift

While the focused messaging for Banatrol Plus supported Medtrition's values and desires to help others, the new ads also empowered an entire population who has been suffering with diarrhea. With their new framework, messaging, and focus, Medtrition is getting customer responses like this:

> *"Banatrol Plus gets me and what it is like to be a chronic sufferer of diarrhea. My digestive system feels like a battle zone and products like Imodium shut my gut down temporarily but eventually I need to turn it back on again. To have a natural solution that works with my body has been a godsend and I am able to get back to having my life."*

Now that is a direct hit on target!

Comment from David Marks, CEO, Medtrition

"I have had Doug work on a few of our brands and the impact is always transformational. As soon as Doug called out that we were being Feature Listers, I could immediately see it and knew we needed to change. With his customer analysis we saw how we were not reaching the chronic sufferer we wanted so we switched to focus on the IBS-D population, which is a very large audience who will give us the highest lifetime value per customer. The evolution of the messaging framework was spot on for the target audience and we are now rolling that out to much greater rewards."

CHAPTER TWELVE

THE DAY JOBBER

———— ■ ————

Those in **Day Jobber** mode are busy doing today what they did the day before, which is also what they will be doing tomorrow. One day blends into the next in a list of daily repetitive tasks that need to get done. These businesses may be stable and comfortable for years, doing about the same revenue year over year. They may use some promotional tactics or advertising consistently that is also in a set routine. They rely on relationships to support the business rather than marketing. These are businesses largely on autopilot, and many of these individuals enjoy doing what they do more than selling what they do.

Mind Trap Issues:
- You can be in Day Jobber mode for years if your business has a steady customer base.
- Day Jobbers are vulnerable to escalating costs or disruptors who figure out how to incorporate innovation to upgrade the customer experience and win more business.

- In most cases, businesses need to continue to grow and/or innovate or they will eventually die. Methods, materials, or facilities will ultimately become outdated.
- An old saying is very applicable to the Day Jobber Mind Trap: "If you are not growing, you're dying." Many Day Jobbers don't figure out that they need to change until it is too late.

Natural Habitats

Those in Day Jobber mode are often present in long-standing local businesses that have grown complacent due to a steady income stream and have turned on their autopilot. They may simply not know what they could do differently. Or, perhaps, they have tried to branch out to do different things in the past, but those efforts failed or lost money so they returned to what was familiar.

Think of your local dry cleaner, independent restaurant, real estate agency, machine shop, professional services firm, construction company, tire shop, preschool, printing shop, or retailer that has been around a long time. Day Jobbers will also include any company that has been overdue for an overhaul but hasn't changed a bit. Taxi companies were in the Day Jobber Mind Trap and were disrupted by Lyft and Uber.

VO Mechanical Case Study

When I walked into VO Mechanical in Ogden, Utah, the first thing I noticed was the lack of decor. VO is one of the largest and most well-reputed mechanical contractors in the area, but their whole demeanor could be described as modestly confident. Their website and even conversations I had with their leadership exuded these same qualities. Nothing flashy, they just let their good work speak for itself. The company thrived and grew because they did exceptionally good metal and plumbing work and were extremely relationship-focused with their clients, often putting client priorities ahead of their own. This meant they had many satisfied customers, many word-of-mouth referrals, and almost no sales materials to speak of.

The Before Picture

VO wanted to scale their operations further, create a steadier stream of business opportunities to add stability for their labor force, and trade out difficult client relationships with ones they loved. They had taken the step to bring on someone to help the company attract new business. Their hire was energetic with a great attitude, but with little historical sales and marketing experience.

The second thing I noticed was there was abundant evidence of the Day Jobber Mind Trap, and it was working against them by creating a brutal annual sales cycle. In general, they were very busy but typically there came a time each year when things were slow and the pipeline started looking uncomfortably weak. They responded by reaching out to their breadth of relationships or pursued lower-yield street bids where they ended up competing against 15 other contractors.

These endeavors turned into work, but it was stressful, time-consuming, lower margin, and just not very fun. Our objective was to assemble a brand, business, and sales framework that would emerge into a process with reliable, highly desirable, higher margin, higher happiness workflow to replace those more stressful times of the year.

The After Picture with the Rise Framework

When we asked the VO Mechanical team my first workshop question, "If you were to encounter a prospect who knew nothing about your company and you wanted to tell them up to three things why they should work with you instead of someone else, what would you say?" I was looking, as I always do, for how consistent or inconsistent the company lens is about itself and also how distinctive its leadership sees itself in relation to top competitors.

VO's answers were predictable and relatively consistent around the following themes.

"I would tell the prospect we do high quality work with a great deal of craftsmanship, that we meet our deadlines, and that we don't nickel and dime them with change orders."

While the statement did provide accurate information about what they did and how they worked, the problem with this pitch was that it was not only identical to what every one of their competitors would say; it was also completely generic language. As a business that was focused and busy with their day-to-day efforts of bidding and completing projects, it was honestly natural for the team to merely explain the work they did and how they did it.

As Day Jobbers, they had never reflected or considered that those messages would be indistinguishable from competitors. And while the VO team may have felt their craftsmanship was better than others, customers were already expecting quality. Thus, VO's self-assessed top qualities were just blending in like a commodity, adding a Copy Catter quality to their message if ever questioned.

Since distinctive attributes were difficult for VO's team to identify, I talked to eight VO Mechanical clients. As part of the questioning, I asked clients what things VO did well and what they could do better. In this case, VO Mechanical was consistently identified as handling more complex projects and doing them with incredible precision.

VO Mechanical's customers viewed them this way:

- They did their work quickly and efficiently.

- They minimized downtime for the facility.
- They stood by the quality of their work.
- They did what was needed instead of sticking strictly to the specifications.
- They worked well with other contractors in a leadership role.
- They used technology well to prevent onsite problems.
- They had a great set of pre-fabrication capabilities so more work could be completed onsite.

Something happened in those conversations that had never occurred in all my years of doing this work. When asked what they could improve, over half of the clients indicated that they could not think of one thing VO Mechanical could do better. At first, I took that as a nice knee-jerk response, so I probed from multiple angles asking about specific project elements and stages. Even with that detailed prompting, they could not think of incremental improvements. This gem became a very important part of VO's Rise Framework. With these new insights, VO went from being a tired version of every other mechanical contractor to literally being the best in the industry and Claiming their own Mountain. Wow!

We Plan for Perfection

The VO Way

We Act Like We Own It

Lifetime Relationship Builders

Given the client information and feedback, there were two substantial areas of unmet needs in the market with white space for improvement. The first was commitment. While there are several subcontractors who do good work, the magnitude of commitment could be higher. The second unmet need was offering clients long-term, trusted partnerships. VO Mechanical found an organic path to build these relationships by starting with some small service jobs for a new client. The great work they would undoubtedly do with that job would lead to additional service jobs, and as that trust grew, more complicated larger project opportunities would emerge.

Rather than being casual or incidental about this, the opportunity for VO Mechanical was to identify the desired client relationships, then do whatever was necessary to start winning service work. VO Mechanical could then articulate that their way of doing business was built around lifetime relationships. They could tell clients, "We know your buildings as well or better than you do, so we can always be there to do the right thing regardless of the nature of the need." Their commitment and outstanding track record would provide clients with a trusted partner they could rely on.

Promise: We Plan for Perfection

We landed on the Promise of *We Plan for Perfection*. We purposefully did not go so far as to claim perfection because that would be over the line of being both arrogant and unrealistic. The Promise does set the stage, though, for a bunch of yummy things that VO Mechanical could own. The first wonderful thing this Promise accomplishes is that it prompts immediate questions from potential clients: "What do you mean by that?" or, "How do you do that?" This then gives the seller the opportunity to tell the VO story, which is where the Pillars, Proof Points, and Power Plant come into play. It also manifested its way into putting the VO Mechanical logo on key systems at the completion of the build.

Other companies might put a sticker on the work to call in the case of need for maintenance. The VO Mechanical stamp means excellence in project execution and when the team places this at the end of the project, it means this work was done as close to perfect as possible and it is a badge of honor.

Pillar 1: The VO Way. This Pillar is the process the company follows to produce near-perfection. This is also how we translated a generic-sounding term of "we do quality work" into something powerful and distinctive. It gives the seller the ability to convey a compelling story that includes everything from hiring, to training, to process, to work in the field, to technology and fabrication talents. They even built their own app to speed workflow and enhance superior collaboration within the team. BIM is a problem detection software that helps identify potential risks in the field before they are built and VO Mechanical is a leading expert in its use. The seller can elaborate on or shorten the explanation of these qualities as time permits.

Pillar 2: We Act Like We Own It. One of the things that stood out for VO Mechanical was that they placed client needs above themselves . . . in a very real, very substantiated way, VO Mechanical would absolutely do whatever was necessary to deliver exceptional work on time, even if the client was the one to introduce unforeseen obstacles. *They delivered as if they owned it.* As if their own life and self-worth depended on the success of delivering each day. This Emotional Pillar allows storytelling that begins with how they do bids where they plan for what is needed, not just what is specified. They also build not only for how the equipment in the building needs to perform today, but also with a thoughtfulness for their client's future needs. It enables VO to talk about their processes for minimizing downtime and management at the site, which they are so good at.

Pillar 3: Lifetime Relationship Builders. This Relationship Pillar involves an expression of scarcity and the importance of shared appreciation for each party in the relationship. It also dials up what had been done anecdotally with clients in the past, emphasizing VO's intention from the beginning to do both the smaller service work and the big projects. Service work and service contracts are great for VO because they are a steadier stream of revenue relative to the big project engagements. Service work also acts to gain early awareness and access to future projects, increasing the probability of competing against a few or no competitors instead of the street fight when 15 competitors are all putting out their lowest cost bid.

We built the framework to reflect the truth of what VO Mechanical meant to the hearts and minds of its clients. By incorporating the best of their assets, available market white space, and the intention of what the business should seek to become, VO Mechanical had a strong plan for success. VO has graciously allowed us to provide more information from their framework. It is my hope that these details will help you better visualize how to create your own Rise Framework.

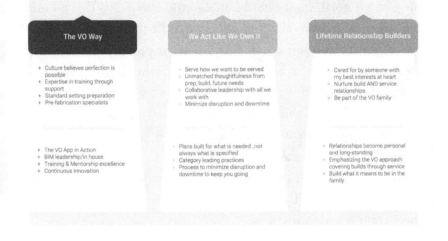

Targeting Impact

Incrementally, VO Mechanical's efforts to remedy their Mind Trap acted as the catalyst to drive targeting decisions. Now they have a clear understanding of the real, impactful, and near-perfect service they offer to clients, and are building up all the details necessary to allow them to Claim the Top of the Mountain in their space. They also have a plan to gain better clients and consistent work. Instead of chasing bids to fill the pipeline, they aligned on a priority of targeting vertical markets in clean manufacturing and healthcare, both areas in which VO Mechanical excels in geographies best suited to their labor force.

Through a More, Poor, and Core customer analysis completed by Victoria Sassine, they established that only five percent of their revenue was associated with "Poor" clients they would like to replace. Going in, they had estimated that about 20 percent of clients were Poor, which is what consistently happens. Clients who are painful to work with take on a disproportionate presence in your emotional psyche. Winding down those relationships that leave the team feeling unappreciated and depleted ends up being a great emotional boost for the company. This allows the time to intentionally find clients that fit the desired criteria. With these enhancements, nurturing a more public presence with greater awareness of their undisputed leadership in their arena is easily established.

VO Mechanical shifted to a more focused outreach with a specific pathway of moving from maintenance relationships to full relationships and became seriously focused on the prospecting process. They landed two big new accounts quickly and worked through a process of transitioning out those accounts that left them feeling undervalued.

Culture Shift

In full transparency, in the beginning, some of the members of the team were less comfortable using the descriptions we came up with for their Rise Framework. It was a rather foreign way of describing the business, and to these Day Jobbers it smelled like *selling* which was an ugly word for them. So, they were less enthusiastic to embrace this new way of talking about their business. The key was breaking down the messaging into bite-size chunks that were more palatable because they were ultimately the truth of what and how the company already operated. We were, in effect, simply providing more consistent and detailed language relative to the quality and craftsmanship they were already talking about.

This was a wonderful win for everyone involved as the framework created a clear, incremental path to an inspiring destiny. This is super important . . . to have a path that can be realized based on the resources already available. There is no point of creating a grand plan that cannot be executed. The goal is not to rework or redefine who companies are. The goal is to figure out the most valuable assets the entity has, elevate them even further to be ahead of competition, and then articulate and build operations and Proof Points that reflect the best of who they are.

For VO Mechanical, nothing about their day-to-day work changed. They were still going to continue to work toward perfection on every project, for every client. They didn't change their management team or introduce a new employee incentive structure. They didn't even add anything to the walls! But the massive change was how the VO team was now unified in how they viewed themselves. The client testimonials revealed that they were already a powerhouse in their industry—and they could finally see it and present it in a way to attract more new clients.

Comments from VO Mechanical President, Joshua Van Orden

"I wasn't completely sure what I was signing up for when we undertook this process as I have never done something like this before. I can tell you it surpassed my expectations. We did not have a formalized method for prospecting, but I knew we wanted to elevate our game. The business goal was to have an updated approach to building a client list, which gives us the strong and steady work that makes the lives of our team more dependable. With Doug and Victoria, we also completed a More, Poor, and Core analysis of our entire client and prospect base, which is focusing our efforts on where we get the greatest ROI. We used to sound like everyone else, but now we break out from the rest of the pack. We are making more money and feeling more fulfilled in our relationships. This work is powerful!"

CHAPTER THIRTEEN
THE TACTICIAN

———————

Those in the **Tactician** Mind Trap look at their list of personal strengths or company assets and, like any good businessperson, thinks about how they can continue to grow and build revenue through new tactics. The challenge is that the short-term tactics to expand the business are often isolated relative to prior tactics and do not add up to a broader conclusion about brand purpose and position. The tactics may not be fully baked and synced with a great overall mission, so they include flaws that prevent them from having their desired impact when they were launched. Those in Tactician mode will often confuse tactics for strategies.

Mind Trap Issues:
- Tacticians hope the next promotion, the next piece of equipment, the next salesperson, the next new product, the next new hire, the next target outreach will be the one to move the business forward.
- There is a cycle Tacticians fall into that they are unaware of:

1. New tactic is identified.
2. Hope is built to justify investment.
3. Resources are dedicated.
4. Tactic fails to materialize sufficiently.
5. Loss of interest and investment.
    . . . and the cycle repeats.

Tactician Cycle

- Nearly every business has some Tactician qualities because we are all faced with the need to generate new ideas to help grow the business. Some tactics will succeed in helping to drive incremental revenue. This is not a zero-sum game.

- The struggle continues because life is continually about coming up with the next idea to grow because the last idea did not yield what they hoped it would.
- The challenge with each tactic is they do not add up to a broader meaning of purpose and connection between the seller and the buyer and there is a lack of permanence because each tactic tends to be short lived and more isolated in nature.
- Being in Tactician mode is tiring because they work so hard for what turns out to be modest returns in most cases. Some of those tactics will even require a lingering level of support for old ones while adding new ones to their list of responsibilities.
- Tacticians need a stronger, more powerful overall business strategy or positioning that drives the business forward and provides direction for choosing tactics.

Note: There are research methodologies that can optimize and validate (go/no-go) tactics before they are launched to avoid wasting time and energy on efforts that are not going to pay out. We are big fans of qualitative feedback loops where you draft your best attempt of what you plan to present to the market. Share that with eight to 10 prospects in your target market in a 60-to-90-minute qualitative discussion format. Edit and adjust. Repeat for one to two rounds to build confidence. I have done this process hundreds of times and always increase demand at least 20 percent and often much more. This process can take a dog to a winner if done properly in some cases.

Natural Habitats

Tacticians are often entrepreneurs who have acquired their skills working for a previous employer, are good at what they do, and decide to go out on their own. What Tacticians do not realize when they start their businesses is that it is not enough to be good at your craft. You also have to create your company's overarching strategy that includes marketing, sales, hiring, accounting, etc. Otherwise, you will just be reactive to the next shiny thing you think might help you grow the business.

La Jolla Cosmetic Case Study

Marie Olesen has always been intensely focused on customer service. At the age of 12, she left a comment card at the Disneyland Hotel reporting delays in shuttle service. When the manager responded with a promise to fix the problem, she knew she had a voice. Today she is the owner and CEO of La Jolla Cosmetic, one of the first and largest cosmetic plastic surgery and medical spas in the country that her husband, Merrel, started many years ago as an elite surgeon. I have the good fortune of becoming her friend.

Marie is perhaps the most empathetic and customer centric business owner I have ever met. She places enormous importance on client satisfaction and experience. She even created another company called Real Patient Ratings to independently measure client satisfaction and every customer review captured is shared with the entire team. At the time of writing this book, she has collected over 7,500 real reviews from clients. Many places manipulate reviews . . . not Marie, she is the real deal who recognizes you can't fake or cheat your way to greatness.

The Before Picture

La Jolla Cosmetic is a very successful practice. One great thing about the work we do is that no matter how successful a business is, it can become even more successful by going through our Rise Framework approach. La Jolla Cosmetic had their overarching values of teamwork, quality, and great patient experiences. Their improvements have an exceptional history of success and to their credit, many tactics they had pursued were working to grow the practice and strengthen the customer experience. They were the most successful Tacticians I had ever worked with. Most of the time, Tacticians watch many of their attempts fall short of their goals to be replaced by the next idea to win the day.

Where the Tactician quality most shone through for La Jolla Cosmetic was in that, despite the many improvements they made over the years—adding new services, staff, loyalty programs, etc.—from a prospect perspective, their set of offerings was long and overwhelming and branding lacked a singular inspiring conclusion or reason to engage. Marie is always setting the highest bar for herself to be the best and to do the best for those she serves, so she asked if we could help establish that clarity of purpose and meaning along with anything else that might be helpful to the business.

The many tactics pursued over the course of years had given La Jolla Cosmetic an abundance of assets to work with that had not yet had the benefit of being assembled into a cohesive storyline and intentional set of client conclusions. Here are some of the individual assets to their credit:

- The tremendous heritage and legacy of being one of the first cosmetic surgery centers in the US, going back to 1988. They train many surgeons.
- A self-contained, on-site surgery center

- Never-ending pursuit of having a full suite of best-in-class services
- Outstanding practices, people, and procedures
- 100 percent customer-centric mindset
- "Best of San Diego" winners for 19 out of the last 20 years
- The Glam-Fam customer loyalty program
- A cohesive team across the surgery center and medical spa
- Advanced patient outcome visualization technologies

One of the things I also found most inspiring about La Jolla Cosmetic was that they talked about how they loved their patients and wanted them to feel loved during every interaction with the team, but they wanted this feeling to come through more strongly. La Jolla Cosmetic was amazing for those prospects who knew what procedure they wanted. If they had progressed that far into the purchase funnel, they were meticulously attended to through the processes of receiving those procedures and services. All those conversion metrics were tracked, reported, and optimized every month throughout the business. My concern was for the top of the purchase funnel. For those who did not know what procedure they wanted, they had to do their own homework and figure that out on their own. This process could be overwhelming, potentially alienating, and could take them away from La Jolla Cosmetic.

This is true of all cosmetic surgery centers and medical spas because they tune into the procedures they provide, but not so much into what would get a prospect to the point of choosing a surgery. This is a common Mind Trap. By providing a long list of procedures, La Jolla Cosmetic is thinking in the first person, "Here is a list of what we do," instead of thinking what the process must be like for the potential client who might feel overwhelmed.

The unmet need was to create a stronger, more curated pathway for a prospect to quickly go from a recognized need to a visualized outcome with the fewest friction points. In other words, a prospective client who merely knew they didn't like the extra skin around their eyes or the extra fat on their thighs needed a guide to help them navigate to the best procedure options for their desired result. And suggesting they should just call a counselor at the clinic does not consider the customer's perspective. Most people view that step as a significant risk where they may be manipulated into a purchase that is not in their best interest or that they may feel embarrassed or ashamed of their situation.

We began with the recognition that an important unmet need for La Jolla Cosmetic would be to elevate the speed and ease of learning the best alternatives to serve a client's desires with the ability to confidently visualize their own personal "after picture." This would be valuable to drive both conversion rates and the speed of the purchase decision cycle.

The other big white space for La Jolla Cosmetic and the industry was the concept of love itself. The label of "plastic" surgery inherently connotes a shallowness on the part of the client. As a team, we hated that term and were drawn to the concept of being on the opposite side of this association—to be the defender of those who desire these services. If you step into the heart and head of the client, they see something about their physical appearance they would like to change. Much of the world will preach that it is not what is on the outside, but on the inside that matters. That is a whole lot of societal judgment to be coming up against. Plastic surgery could be considered the ultimate act to love yourself so much that you are willing to have a procedure and spend significant money to see yourself in the mirror each day in the way you choose.

The After Picture with the Rise Framework

Marie has allowed me to share many of the details of what we created to help other businesses find their own success. She genuinely seeks to elevate the entire category.

Promise: Where Dreams Become Real

Inside each person who desires a procedure is a dream of a physical appearance they would like to see each day with all the emotional benefits this new look will inspire. This became La Jolla Cosmetic's Promise—they are the destination *Where Dreams Become Real*. This is a Promise that contains both familiar and new language to become an intriguing new Promise.

Where Dreams Become Real for the patient includes the following journey we serve:

- Their interest in cosmetic surgery begins with something that is not satisfying with their body . . . followed by a dream of how it could be different.

- Then the dream becomes informed of possibilities of what could change that. This is a gradual process requiring opinions, education, ideas, prioritization, and ultimately an action, all of which can be supported by La Jolla Cosmetic.

- A hope that they can have a safe, no-judgment exploration of their dream with a staff member in a safe place to explore. This leads to appointments, procedures, and ongoing relationships.

- The dream to see the "after picture" prior to having the procedure done is where the dream starts to become real.

- And then after the procedure . . . the dream is real. The dream is delivered.

La Jolla Cosmetic had all the goods to deliver on the Promise with room to further develop this conclusion for a lifetime. Great Promises reflect the best of what the business is today, but also what it can become. That La Jolla Cosmetic is the place where dreams are explored and then become real became the centralizing theme of the entire practice.

The Pillars underneath the Promise needed to provide a logical organizing construct from which La Jolla Cosmetic could convey their story. Without this framework, the business could be quite confusing and disjointed for a prospect. Three Pillars formed around: 1) Our Practice, 2) Our People, and 3) Our Process, each with baked-in flexibility to tell a compelling story in 30 seconds, three minutes, 30 minutes, or three hours, depending on the nature of the conversation they were involved in. The framework also created flexibility to zero in on one Pillar relative to another—again depending upon the interest of the audience and time available.

Pillar 1: Our Practice—Always Leading. La Jolla Cosmetic's Emotional Pillar needed to elevate the considerable heritage and excellence the practice had achieved. In this Pillar they could talk about being the first cosmetic surgery center. But being the first has limited value or could even be a negative (viewed as outdated) if you do not do more with it. In this case, their legacy included winning Best Cosmetic Surgery Group of San Diego for 19 out of the last 20 years and Best Cosmetic Medical Spa + Best Weight Loss Clinic for the past eight years.

They could also start touting being the practice where other surgeons come to learn using the latest and best tools to be certain the message was viewed as leading and not outdated as a result of being the oldest. They also have exceptional staff and provider retention rates to support this Pillar.

Pillar 2: Our People—Where Empathy Meets Excellence. This Relationship Pillar highlighted La Jolla Cosmetic's use of end-to-end Board-Certified individuals to maximize safety and care. Perhaps even more valued, one of the training elements we went through was around the concept of *Redefining Professionalism.* La Jolla Cosmetic already completed extensive training for performing procedures exceptionally well. We introduced the data around the loneliness epidemic and asked the question, "What if we liberated the team to focus on the conclusion of the client experience anchored in love rather than just the tactics of the procedure?"

We were a little nervous that the team might feel like the idea of surrounding clients with love and personal care when they interacted with them might feel like crossing a professional boundary. To my delight, the staff felt relieved and liberated to be themselves more and that they could connect in a more human and less transactional way. La Jolla Cosmetic appreciates the entire staff and their role in providing client satisfaction. The new Promise further freed them to express love to the patients and increased the staff's happiness with their roles even further.

Your customers are not the only ones experiencing the loneliness epidemic. Your staff is feeling it as well, and we all are just looking for brave leaders who are willing to create the opening to care and connection for others. Your people might be ready and willing to do this, and they may not. This is certainly not something to be forced.

Pillar 3: Our Process—Visualized Outcomes. This Process Pillar pulls together the white space of improved envisioning capabilities, emergent technology, and before/after picture studies that can help clients picture their new appearance after completing the procedure. The range of technology solutions that can accomplish this varies by procedure, which is fine. The point is not the technology itself. The point is focusing on what would be required to move a client from initial interest to confidence in their own personal after picture as efficiently as possible. This work will continue to be a work in progress as it will leverage new technologies that can help accomplish the end goal.

The full Rise Framework that emerged to pull together branding, sales, targeting, operations, and culture is offered below and Marie has graciously agreed to share it in this book.

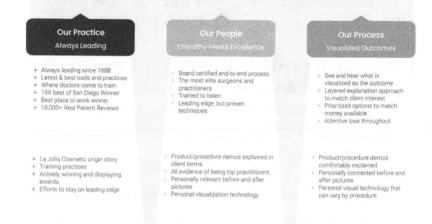

Target Impact

This work became the catalyst to integrate what had previously been handled as two separate but related entities. When we started, La Jolla Cosmetic Surgery Centre and La Jolla Cosmetic Medical Spa were separate, which acted as a barrier to the seamless flow of patients from one set of services to the other. Pulling them together occurred after our workshop as the team revealed the obstacles that separation created.

After launching this new framework, La Jolla Cosmetic brought a more solidified and inspiring vision of itself to the world. Part of conveying their story even more effectively finally put them into winning the award for Top Cosmetic Surgery Center not only in the US, but in the world, from internationally recognized MyFaceMyBody*.

Sales of this very successful practice have grown to an all-time high. Even more importantly to this leadership team is that an already winning culture improved even further. Marie loves the feedback from the team, that they feel more at ease to be themselves, and that this engagement is bolstering conversion rates, retention rates, and employee satisfaction.

Culture Shift

As described previously, La Jolla Cosmetic was already well versed and committed to supporting their clients. Their Rise Framework unifies their team to be more genuine and is now being used to support the onboarding of every new employee conveying clarity on the standards with which they choose to operate. The most powerful shift was the awareness the service providers had. By shifting from the emphasis on excellence in procedures to nurturing the conclusion they sought to create where their clients would feel loved and appreciated, everyone was happier and service providers felt more liberated to be themselves and have a deeper connection with their clients.

Comments from Marie Olesen, CEO, La Jolla Cosmetic

"We just celebrated our 33rd anniversary in business and are having our best year ever. This is not an exaggeration when I tell you that I consider Doug to be one of the most important people I have ever met. We have always been the leader in our market, but in retrospect we have never had a cohesive approach to running and talking about our business. I'm very customer centric and we share every review with our entire office. But even with that, you don't realize how you can lose perspective of what it is like being your customer when you are busy doing your job every day. I didn't understand the limitations of our tactical approach because we had never considered that our initiatives were a bit like chasing the next shiny object.

"Doug brought that lens back to us at the highest level and then packaged it so we have a better approach on how best to perform in every area of our company. Most importantly our team and our patients are happier. It's a joy to behold. We are so grateful for Doug's intervention. He has a special gift, and we feel very fortunate to have benefitted from his insights and intuition."

CHAPTER FOURTEEN
THE DEFENDER

Those in the **Defender** Mind Trap express a great deal of confidence in their own judgment and choices above those around them. Sometimes this is because they have a strong and experienced background in their category, and sometimes it is because they are just wired that way. Defenders often convince themselves they are good listeners when in fact their time spent in discussions is explaining themselves—either why they made the decisions they did or why all your good suggestions are things they have already thought of but have not had the time or resources to reach yet.

Mind Trap Issues:
- Sources of ideas to improve the business are limited to those in Defender mode and the inner circle of confidants who tend to agree with them.
- Employees can become "yes people" more interested in protecting their job than the best interests of the company.
- May experience high turnover and blame those either out or on their way out.

- May blame customers for "not getting it," not appreciating that it is the responsibility of the company to respond to the impressions of prospects, and not the other way around.
- Those with the Defender Mind Trap feel successful if they are right and like failures if they are wrong. The challenge is many will never know they have slipped into this Mind Trap because of a guarded ego.

Note: It may be hard to recognize yourself acting as a Defender. You may need an outsider to open this possibility for you, being careful not to simply ask a "yes person" who may opt for telling you what you want to hear to avoid creating risks for themself.

If this Mind Trap resonates with you, I encourage you to dig to the core underlying reason why you may be in a Defender Mind Trap. This is a personality driven Mind Trap, so there are likely old things you grew up with that are still playing out today. Perhaps you had to fight to be heard and considered when you were a child or were frequently criticized . . . recognize that those old dynamics are not the same as the present-day environment and that you can create anything you choose to experience.

Get people on your team who are capable and convey to them the importance of not simply telling you what you want to hear. Work on being open so you can hear their ideas, even if you do not totally agree.

Those with the Defender Mind Trap particularly need to revisit the points of friction in the sales journey, as they can be more committed to their convictions than their conversions. Use data wherever possible as empirical evidence in a direction that removes emotion.

Then, practice empathy! Extend compassion to your prospect in what is behind their friction points and consider how you might approach this differently.

Everyone should have some Defender qualities. You need to be able to stand up for yourself and justify decisions. It is when the strength of conviction becomes too strong that the Mind Trap can work against your best interests. It can be a fine line sometimes.

Natural Habitats

The Defender Mind Trap can emerge in any category. I have encountered three types of Defenders. Some are just overconfident and don't think they need help. Some confuse strength of conviction for leadership and are unteachable and unmovable in their opinions in order to show control of the situation. And the rest are Defenders because they feel it is their responsibility as a leader to have all the answers and that it is a sign of weakness if they don't.

I do feel sympathy for these individuals. Many are smart and have great ideas, but they literally get in their own way and prohibit their success. When I think of people who operate heavily in defending mode, I imagine they may have grown up in households with parents who made them feel like whatever they did was never enough. I have zero empirical evidence to support that conclusion, but it makes implicit sense to me and I can personally relate to it.

Defender Case Studies

I now avoid working with those who are adamant Defenders who do not seem capable of moving to a growth mindset, but I have in the past. I once invested in a startup company that had developed a new technology that could literally become the new encryption standard in a post-quantum world. Current encryption standards are numerically based with very long combinations of numbers. As computing speeds for computers grow faster, their ability to hack against all possible combinations of numbers also increases. This company developed a non-numeric, algorithmically based approach that may very well have been unbreakable. On top of that, it also required very little computational footprint, which meant it could be used throughout entire systems—even including very small, unprotected sensors. So many opportunities and possibilities! I was sold! But bringing an entirely new encryption technology to market would be difficult.

This was made even harder by having a Defender CEO. He was struggling to package this proposition together to bring to the world. We would get these amazing partnering opportunities that seemed very promising, only to have them die on the doorstep. Rather than learning from these failures and repackaging the solution, the CEO would find problems either with the potential partners being at fault or would turn on the same employees whom he had praised as heroes when they found the prospect in the first place.

He had three tactics that enabled him to stay in power longer than he should have, which wasted considerable resources in the process. The first was that the story of the technology was impressive and was able to attract capital. The second was the fact that it is reasonable and expected that a number of early partner opportunities will fail as a startup company finds its footing in the world. The third was that he had organized the capital structure of the company to have two classes of stock where he could have a controlling interest. And with these tactics behind him, I had the terrible experience of watching this very promising company burn through capital and grow into an increasingly toxic environment.

Employees were faced with a choice of unfailing loyalty to the CEO or a quick and decisive pathway to exiting the company. The potential partnerships failures continued to pile up, but the CEO remained convinced that he was faultless. The only way things were able to change was that the company finally started to run out of money. The technology was still cutting edge and attractive to investors. Thankfully, we were able to find an investor willing to put up five million dollars. But, with the financial track record and failed partnerships, these unbiased investors could see the writing on the wall and would only invest if the company replaced the CEO. The Board was then faced with the decision to either shut down the company or take the money with a new CEO. They rightly chose the latter and the company lived to fight another day.

The Defense for Defenders

One of the things that can make defending a tricky or confusing subject are those social media voices out there that are chanting that all you need to do is just stick with it and don't quit. Hold on just a little longer to your conviction and you will see success. They cite examples of people who were committed in their conviction and, despite setbacks, found success. They say that the difference between winners and losers is that the winners are unmovable in their conviction to succeed.

There is some truth to staying committed to your ideas. You don't want to put yourself into the position of continually pivoting based on the most recent opinion, because that is a no-win situation as well. I find it tricky to define that fine line between focus and being obstinate.

I can appreciate a little Defender in anyone as I believe there should be a natural tendency to stand up for your work. I can slip into Defender mode when I present my work . . . it is human nature. It becomes a problem when it dominates and creates an inability to receive feedback on an ongoing basis.

On occasions when I encounter these individuals and find an opening, I like to convey what I believe is the most important part of being a leader. A great leader is not the one who knows everything and has all the answers. A great leader is someone who knows how to get the very best out of everyone they work with . . . that's it. I have had some success breaking through in these cases when the defensiveness was not driven by arrogance, but rather insecurity.

When you can help those operating in a Defender mode feel safe and reimagine their relationships, then you have a good shot at wearing those barriers down over time. Then you can focus on the other Mind Traps present. But those fully committed to Defending have not had good outcomes. They each either lost their position or their company with time.

So, while having some Defender qualities is necessary to advocate for yourself and your position, err toward empathy for those you serve as clients or employees. Build a trusted advisor network or board you can count on to keep perspective of what will carry your best interests forward.

CHAPTER FIFTEEN
THE GLORIFIER

Those in the **Glorifier** Mind Trap have concluded that surrounding nouns with loftier adjectives when describing their proposition will convince buyers of the wonderfulness of their product and lead to conversion. They create a more elaborate and elevated vision of their offering with clever descriptions they believe will inspire their prospect to a better vision of themselves and the lives they believe they would want to live.

Mind Trap Issues:
- Glorifiers have not realized that people are tired of exaggeration and that every additional adjective signals you are lying or are attempting to manipulate them for personal gain.
- To be even more direct, people are burnt out on much of the generic marketing platitudes that marketers have fallen into using over the years. Those words run hollow today.

- There are both shortened attention spans and a drive toward simplicity in what buyers want to hear about the propositions being presented to them.
- The way to connect is through simple and deeply real intention and service with clarity that your existence is built on your motivation to serve.
- Glorifiers will often have exaggerated preconceived notions of what the lives and motivations are of either what they are providing to the world or who their customer is. As a result, they are often misaligned between desires and realities.
- Glorifying can be inward or outward facing. Inward-facing Glorifiers like to feel very good about their work and their workplace. They avoid being self-critical and choose to believe that what they are bringing to the world is magnificent. The outward-facing Glorifier exaggerates the qualities of their offerings to their prospects, creating perceptions of deceit and mistrust.

Natural Habitats

Outward-facing Glorifiers are often, but not exclusively, involved with luxury or premium-priced brands. Inward-facing Glorifiers can be in any category. Their common trait is they are pleasers and want everyone to feel good about what they are doing. They would rather paint an optimistic story of their greatness than focus on being critical as a means of self-improvement. They can also be in marketing agencies that have fallen into the Mind Trap of seeking to be clever and lofty rather than meaningful and direct.

Brandless Case Study

I recently worked with Brandless out of Salt Lake City. This company was born out of the noble desire of its founders to find and be the answer to providing great, high-integrity products to customers at lower prices. And while pursuing a very worthy cause, they burned through hundreds of millions of invested capital focusing on the idea that there are substantial markups on consumer products that come in the form of "brand taxes." These are costs associated with merchandising, advertising, promotions, distribution, in store shelving allowances, etc.

The Before Picture

The initial concept became, "What if we cut out all those costs and passed them onto customers so they could get great products at better prices? Wouldn't that be valuable?" They had an inspiring leader very capable of promoting that story and they were off to the races!

Around the same time, someone else in the group recognized an additional consumer insight—that more natural, higher integrity ingredients associated with wellness was an important trend. So, that was added to the brand as if it were somehow part of the same thing. The business was launched and gained a reasonable following of customers attracted to the concept, but more growth was needed to fulfill the vision. That triggered a secondary Tactician Mind Trap where they started chasing a set of tactics to grow the business.

They added lots of lines of business—covering food, health and beauty, and household products. Then the company decided they should sell everything at a three-dollar price point aligned with the mission of eliminating the "brand tax." That attracted attention but killed any hopes of profitability. They even chased getting into the travel business.

Under that leadership, Brandless was ultimately forced to shut down and look for an exit. They invited me to work with the new leadership team who was sorting through what to keep, what to evolve, and how. It was fascinating to sift through all their old materials, especially as it gave a glimpse into how their worthy mission really framed how they saw themselves—regardless of any business failures. In truth, I may never have come across a more exaggerated inward-facing group of Glorifiers.

Their library was filled with extensive presentations articulating the grandness of what they were providing the world and their associated importance in providing this much-needed offering. The remarkable thing was it seemed like they were writing all their presentations more to impress each other than their customers.

The contrast between this elaborate internal branding of greatness relative to the customer-facing presentation was remarkable. Their customer-facing material was completely stripped down to generic levels because they were Brandless, after all. They were committed to their community, but packaging couldn't even say "Brandless." This limited them in what they would say around the products, and they lacked reviews because all that was being associated with branding was deemed bad and counter to the "counter-brand." They were Glorifiers whose ideal view of self was not translating to market and it led to a complete turnover in the management team.

The After Picture with the Rise Framework

A big part of what we needed to determine was how to work with the new leadership team to assess what to keep and what to replace in the old Brandless proposition. After all, there were an awful lot of good efforts and intentions spent attracting a sizable following. We landed on the following Promise and Pillars.

Promise: Brand Less. Live More.

We landed on the Promise of *Brand Less. Live More*. We chose this for a number of reasons:

- It ties in the brand name directly while suggesting a better life could be found here.
- It is at the same time familiar and new.
- It can build sub-stories behind it, leveraging "Live More" in different ways by SKU or category.
- It creates a simple equation that implies spending less time with the frivolous and more time in the meaningful which fits with market trends.
- It suggests sustainability without overemphasizing it so Brandless can live outside of limiting "natural only" associations.
- It invites intrigue and a question: "What do you mean by 'Brand Less. Live More'?"
- It can be used with every community Brandless seeks to engage with.
- It is easy to remember and catchy.

**Brand Less.
Live More!**

The "For You"
Portfolio

Wonderful
Products

Community
Lead

Pillar 1: For You. The "For You" Portfolio was established in part to refocus attention on building real connection between product and the customers Brandless serves. This is the Emotional Pillar: everything the company does is intentional to being of service. That means . . .

- Product mix enriches my life daily.
- Portfolio that grows with me over time.
- Always proven to be better for me and the planet.

Pillar 2: Wonderful Products. Wonderful Products is the Process-Oriented Pillar. These are all the things Brandless does to have a consistent deliverable of value across its entire lineup. In other words, having consistency in brand conclusion requires a formula for how products are delivered.

At a product level, the company:

- Takes out the bad (specifically identifying what and why at a SKU level).
- Replaces with the good.
- Makes beautiful and affordable products.

Pillar 3: Community Led. Community Led is the Relational Pillar. As I write this, Brandless is working toward being a community-powered business where products and services are developed in collaboration with customers who choose to make the portfolio an important part of their lives.

This is where we aligned on for this Pillar:

- Community is essential to Brandless life/growth.
- Ambassadorship is actively encouraged and nurtured.
- Portfolio is actively curated with the community.

Brandless would also need a formula that would hold the integrity of its message and offering as it grew and added more items and potential complexity. We needed a framework that would be easy to follow and could be explained super simply:

- Take out the bad.
- Replace with the good.
- Make it beautiful and affordable.

Every SKU could have this simple explanation attached to it for those who want to understand more deeply. Where appropriate the explanation can include:

- These are the ingredients we took out and why.
- These are the ingredients we added and why.

Target Shift

We provided a pretty significant shift in the targeting philosophy as well. The prior administration had adopted this attitudinal segmentation that also suffered from the Glorifier Mind Trap of sounding good but was lacking in true depth to the customers they served. I have done many market segmentations in my life and one of the most common flaws is a subtle but important disconnect between a visualization of a real human you can talk to and connect with at a personal level versus the imaginary persona that sounds clever but is more marketing speak than real.

The target of the future for Brandless is one that wants to be of a community where they find the best of themselves because they are part of a brand that believes in doing good and being good. At Brandless, the community has real power to establish which products and companies are in or out of the portfolio. When you are engaging with the Brandless community, you find and bring the best of yourself, because this is a place where people treasure those sacred times when they can experience the best of humanity.

After we completed the Rise Framework, the business-building strategy of completing acquisitions of over 100 companies was introduced and the branding became an important part of inspiring acquisition targets to become part of the Brandless family.

Culture Shift

Given where the company was coming from, the new administration placed a very high bar on true and meaningful connection to the community. Leadership is highly motivated to keep it real and create an engagement culture in the company that is highly inspired to be closely connected with those they serve in the real world. Hiring is built on it, training is built around it, and even technology development is focused on nurturing this ability.

Comments from Brandless CEO, Cydni Tetro

"Our team was impressed by how quickly Doug was able to dig through all of the history of Brandless, align our vision for the future, and establish a go-forward framework. This business is moving quickly and we needed a partner who could kick start that into high gear. As we evolve to take advantage of new opportunities, we have also been impressed by how Doug is able to offer good insights to win further among our employees, potential investors, customers, and acquisition candidates."

CHAPTER SIXTEEN
THE INTERROGATOR

———————■———————

Those in **Interrogator** mode believe the best way to win the deal is by asking the prospect an excessive number of questions before having earned the right to ask them. The Interrogator convinces himself or herself this is the best way to approach selling because they equate asking lots of questions with being customer centric. They do this because they think it's the best way to identify how to speak the prospect's language. I believe it is also because they neither feel comfortable nor confident in their ability to deliver an elevator pitch that will engage them in further conversation.

Getting out of Interrogator mode requires being able to convey the value proposition with an introduction to how their offering elevates the life of the people who get to experience it. Prospects want to hear this at a high level from anyone who is selling them something. Interrogators also can share something about themselves, connecting to love of the company they are working for and/or the products they provide, a common history with the prospect, or love of what they do to be engaging to create connections that help them to earn the right to ask questions. When the prospect engages, the salesperson can elevate questioning in a respectful and reciprocating manner that feels more like friendship than salesmanship.

This and the Schmoozer are the sales-only Mind Traps. They do not live at a company level, only at a personal level during sales engagement.

Mind Trap Issues:

- Of course, asking questions is good and necessary for good salesmanship. It's when the initial discussion is dominated with excessive questioning that you are in Interrogator mode.
- If you look closer, the questions Interrogators ask are inspired to make the salesperson more comfortable than the prospect.
- The prospect instantly recognizes the salesperson is planning to use this information to manipulate them into buying.
- While some prospects are okay with accommodating the inquiries, most resent the salesperson who has not earned the right to request this information, even if they don't show it.
- A clear version of why their offering matters in the world is not conveyed with an authentic version of the before and after picture of a life lived better once their product is in it.
- There is no consistent brand positioning across the company because every pitch is a one-off. Interrogators are often not confident in their pitch.
- Interrogators leave themselves out as individuals contributing to the engagement. People want to buy from people they like.

- Interrogators miss that good sales questioning occurs through creating a state of escalating reciprocity where the salesperson offers some vulnerability into who and what they are, which in turn invites the prospect to open as well. Give vulnerability to get it.

Natural Habitats

Falling into Interrogator mode can happen in any category where there is direct human sales engagement and commissions are involved. I have found them in every category where these dynamics exist.

Jake's Case Study

Jake was in his late twenties. He had broad shoulders and brown, conservatively cut hair. He smiled when he looked at you but stopped when he looked away. Since starting his job at a commercial solar company six years prior, he had been a mid-tier performer—just blending into the pack. He never stood out for any major successes, but since he had never stood out for any major failures either, management just left him alone to do his thing.

The Before Picture

I had the opportunity to witness Jake pitching a prospective client in a 30-minute Zoom call. Here is how it went:

- After a very brief exchange of pleasantries about the weather and the amount of time Jake had been working for the solar company, Jake told the prospect that he wanted to "be efficient" with time and went directly into question mode.
- "*How much do you know about solar?*" Without knowing it, Jake had already put his prospect on defense in the very

first question. For Jake, this was an innocent question to help shape the dialogue. For the prospect, however, it was a no-win inquiry, leaving them to think, "If I don't know much, this salesperson is going to attempt to take advantage of my innocence. But if I know too much, he is going to attempt to see who he is up against and I'm not yet prepared to share that information. Also, it is none of his business how much I know!"

- Next question: *"What are you looking to accomplish with solar on your property?"* Another bad question. The prospect is obviously seeking to save money on their electricity bill. This question is too general without purpose and Jake has put the property owner on the defensive with the risk that he might not answer with the information Jake is looking for . . . and again, to what end?

- Questioning continued . . . *"How much have you been looking into putting solar onto your property?"* This is a premature ask that enables Jake to again see whom he was up against rather than helping the prospect.

- *"How soon are you looking to make a decision?"* Another premature question that sends the signal to the customer that you as the salesperson are going to tune in harder and faster if the prospect has a faster timeline and tune out if the decision is further into the future.

- And of course, the next question . . . *"Who would be involved in making the decision?"* At this point I was personally thinking, "Jake, are you kidding me?" From the prospect's perspective, "I don't have a clue on whether I would want to work with you or not . . . you are getting way ahead of me."

The rest of the conversation did not go that well as the prospect was on the defensive from the start and also seemed to share the feeling that Jake did not know how to sell very well. When Jake finally came to his pitch, he shared how solar was good for saving money and good for the planet and that his company was a leading solar developer in the area. He showed pictures of multiple projects the company had completed. The prospect also talked briefly about the nature of their property, which Jake pulled up on Google Maps. Turns out Jake was not only an Interrogator, but also a Copy Catter because nearly every solar company presents that exact same story!

During the next steps discussion at the end of the 30 minutes, the prospect indicated they would talk internally about next steps and declined Jake's invitation to set a date for a follow-up meeting. They never responded to any of Jake's subsequent follow-ups. I wish I could say this was rare, but I run into this Mind Trap all the time.

Like so many others, Jake is much more comfortable asking questions than talking about the company or himself. He never took the time to consider that many of his prospects might not like his progressive questioning approach. So, he continued in the same ways because he was getting some sales and simply assumed this was his close rate without contemplating another way. Sales leadership had no awareness of this Mind Trap previously, so they never thought to suggest another way either.

Jake lost prospects and lowered his overall conversion rate by alienating prospects who were not okay with him asking questions he had not earned the right to ask. Moreover, Jake had left his camera off the entire time, voiding the prospect with any real human connection.

We might summarize the before picture with Jake as an Interrogator who turned off clients by asking too many questions selling a solar company that blended in with everyone else because they were Copy Catters. I love it! So much upside opportunity!

The After Picture with the Rise Framework

We needed a better story about his solar company (since Jake has moved on to a bigger and higher paying company, we will leave out their name) as well as a better story for Jake. It seems like every solar company sells themselves the same way . . . "Solar is good for the planet and will save you money and here are pictures of projects we have done." If you step into the shoes of the prospect, however, that leaves some pretty big gaps. Prospects think:

- "You may have done these other projects, but how do I know you are going to do *my* specific project well? I am not everyone else."
- "How do I know if I am going to like working with you and your team . . . will I like these people?"
- "Is this going to suck up a whole bunch of my time and be intrusive on our daily activities?"
- "What about long-term support?"
- "How do I know I am getting the best deal with you?"

We immediately went to work on building out the story of the solar company. We knew we needed:

- A tight and distinctive value proposition that could expand or contract with the time available to the prospect.
- Humanize Jake. Turn on the camera! A blank screen is such a wasted opportunity to create a more human connection!
- Add some personal details about Jake early in the conversation to be likeable he could choose from. Love for what

he does. Love of his company, his product, or something he had in common with prospects.

- Eliminate unintended risk elements to the customer journey.

We built a great Rise framework for Jake that his company ultimately adopted for great gain. In the process, we distinguished his solar company from others in the category, preemptively eliminated risk factors to engagement, and humanized the relationship. We built a structure for Jake that enabled him to put an equal emphasis on the brand, critical features, and him.

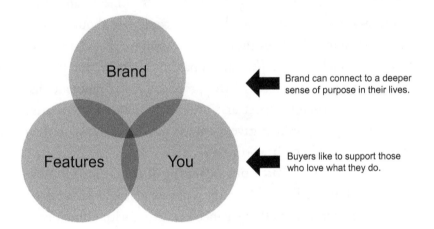

Brand can connect to a deeper sense of purpose in their lives.

Buyers like to support those who love what they do.

Promise: We Realize Your Solar Potential

We landed on a Promise of *We Realize your Solar Potential.* As a Promise, this means we make it about the client and their property first fulfilling what is possible for them through the best ways possible. Within this Promise are the three Pillars that cover Process, People, and Relationships. Each has its corresponding Proof Points and Power Plant.

Pillar 1: Maximizing Your Project. Maximizing Your Project was the Process Pillar where they could talk about the specific tools and techniques they used to optimize the solution for each individual project. This encompassed the inspection process that considered all aspects of the property and equipment that could be optimized for space and need. It also covered alternative financing approaches that gave them the best deal relative to their cash position and credit worthiness.

Pillar 2: Team You Love Working With. Team You Love Working With packaged all of the folks who would be working on their project in ways that balanced expertise with humanity. It also conveyed how they would minimize the time requirements of the client. Pictures and videos of the team were easily accessible. They conveyed a balance of experience, customized expertise at a property level, and niceness. We wanted the prospect to conclude that each person on the team would be someone they would be comfortable engaging with in any situation.

Pillar 3: There for the Long Term. There for the Long Term offset a general weakness in the category where too many solar companies install and abandon. Jake was able to talk about superior monitoring and support systems and with readily available references who could attest to long-term support. These were Proof Points that this would be a system and team that would not leave them with problems down the road.

Personal Story

Next, we worked on building Jake's story. He shared just a little about his humble and hardworking beginnings and explained his personal interest in solar power. He shared that he had chosen solar because he wanted to do his part of being on the right side of doing the good things in the world. He also expressed how he loved working for this particular solar company because of the values they held in serving both clients and employees. It was warm and genuine, held appropriate levels of vulnerability, and gave prospects the opportunity to connect with Jake on a personal level.

We had Jake practice telling his story five times internally, then we gave him feedback on five subsequent Zoom pitches. It felt awkward for Jake at first and his tendency to go back to being an Interrogator was definitely a personal challenge. But he started seeing himself through his prospect's eyes and the more he did that, the more natural it became, and the more confidence he gained. It was working and his conversion for turning leads into closed deals rose dramatically to the point where he was picked up by a competitive solar company.

Jake increased his conversion rates and became the top seller for his solar company, nearly doubling the money he was making previously. Because solar is so fragmented, both companies embraced this very similar Rise Framework, weaving in their own unique spins into it. Since Jake is our client who hired us to help his professional fortunes, we are focusing on the impact we had for him. The reality is sales and margins for both companies increased substantially.

Culture Change

Jake shared with us how the cultures of each company shifted as a result of these adjustments he was able to nurture from moving from a transaction-focused to a relational mindset. They shifted focus in the sales meetings from solely being about numbers related to funnel metrics to include elements related to what they were doing to convey unique benefits they were introducing in their proposals relative to competition. The culture was unified in moving in this direction.

Comments from Jake

"I always thought asking questions of my prospects was the best thing to do as I was listening to my customer. It never occurred to me that this might be a turnoff to people. Many people on my team worked the same way. I always thought to myself, *I will listen to them and then customize my message to be what they would need to hear.*

"After going through the Rise process, I now understand the value of balancing the pitch to incorporate the brand and myself at a level that allows the prospect to have a sense of what they should be looking for in working with us from the beginning. This also makes it easier for me to build the story out in ways that are believable and inspiring. With dedication to this process and with smarter CRM efforts that reinforce our Rise Framework, my sales are up 75 percent and leadership at my new company looks for me to train others."

CHAPTER SEVENTEEN

THE SCHMOOZER

Those in **Schmoozer** mode rely on their ability to be likable or create situations where the salesperson gives the prospect freedom to take a break from the daily grind with cocktails, dinner, a trip, some golf, etc. They rely on relationships to sell, and for those who are good at it, this can work well. My experience with Schmoozers is they get hired by companies who are impressed with the networks of individuals they know, and because the relationships are friend based, the company anticipates that getting to a close is going to be easy.

The reality is that the number and strength of relationships that Schmoozers actually have relative to what you hope they have as a business owner can be difficult to discern during the hiring process. We have also found it is important to be clear about the amount and nature of organizational support that will be needed by the Schmoozer before bringing them into the company. Many are highly focused on their relational qualities at the expense of technical or systems proficiency.

Mind Trap Issues:

- Many who act in Schmoozer mode are heavily committed to a relationship-focused approach at the expense of all others. It can become the only way they feel comfortable selling.
- In the mind of the Schmoozer, getting a warm and friendly appointment set is their job, requiring their unique finesse and networks to make it happen.
- Schmoozers can be overly dependent on other people in their company to do things for them. They might require other staff members to write emails and proposals, provide technical support for even small computer issues, and look for company leadership to finish closing the sale with or for them.
- Being a Schmoozer only becomes problematic if you overly rely on relationships at the expense of product and branding. Why? Because not all prospects want to be wined and dined.
- A Schmoozer might get past the gatekeeper only to get shut down by the ultimate decision-maker, who may view schmoozing as eroding the integrity of a business deal. It is important to be able to adapt to the personality traits your prospect wants to engage with.

Natural Habitats

Schmoozers are present in higher ticket categories where entertaining clients is a common practice and commission sales are the standard.

My Personal Experience with a Schmoozer

Everybody loved Dave. If he walked into a room, he always seemed to know at least one person. And if he didn't, it would not take him long to strike up a conversation. He was fun to be around, told outrageous, super-entertaining stories, and was just the kind of positive guy you want to be around. But Dave drove me nuts. I hired him to our sales team largely because of his charisma, but, more importantly, because he was well connected. He had this amazing network that he had grown over years, and for sales, that can be a huge advantage.

We thought Dave would go out right away and start selling to his connections with ease. He would sporadically assert himself and did help us connect into new relationships that became worth millions of dollars to the company over time. And for that I was grateful. At the same time, I was extremely frustrated by the amount of hand holding he needed. He couldn't write proposals and was not particularly good at emails or following up. But while he would make the introductions and get first meetings, he didn't . . . he couldn't . . . close the deal. I often found myself feeling like if Dave only asserted himself, his impact for the company could be so much larger, with his lack of work ethic continually grating on me. Dave was a quintessential Schmoozer.

We tried to focus on Dave's ability to do this for our company—and he did introduce us to some of the most important relationships the firm has ever had. Most notably, he introduced me to my dear friend Dr. James Taylor, who built our Wealth and Affluence practice, and connected us to American Express, Activision, and others that each became million-dollar-plus annual relationships for us. I knew Dave near the beginning of my career and I wish I had understood his Mind Trap then as well as I do now. Schmoozers can be great assets if you know how to harness their power.

Amy's Case Study

Now in her late forties, Amy had worked in the private aviation space for what was approaching two decades. Like Dave, she had a great network. She also loved jets and over time had assembled a significant network of individuals she would casually list in conversations. I won't say that she was an intentional name-dropper, but I do know when employers at other aviation companies heard her in conversation the little cash register in their minds would ring and they would want to hire Amy.

Because private aviation is a long sales cycle, and because Amy would make introductions into her network, she would stay at each company for a few years before things would fizzle out as leads were not turning into sales and Amy would beat them to the punch moving on to her next company. But this reputation was starting to catch up to her, and so she enlisted us to help her as a personal client. Amy was a Schmoozer with a secondary Feature Lister Mind Trap.

The Before Picture

Amy and Dave were the same person in many ways. Because she was engaging and her prospective clients were friends, sales conversations would circle around and around without moving to a close. Everyone had lots of fun in the process during the early days, but over time, employers do need to make money from their salespeople.

Amy didn't like playing by the same rules as everyone else with things like tracking her leads in Salesforce. She would look for help responding to emails and proposals more than her coworkers and seemed to have more technical challenges even with things like Zoom. At first, these qualities were sort of entertaining. But after enough time passes without enough sales, the fun is not so funny, and relationships start to get strained, leading to receptiveness to the next career move.

Amy was starting to catch onto herself and wanted a new take on an old Mind Trap. As we talked, Amy immediately recognized herself as a Schmoozer and Feature Lister. We used this new self-awareness to help form Amy 2.0.

The After Picture

Helping Schmoozers understand a company's Brand Promise, Pillars, Proof Points, and Power Plants helps them to create deeper relationships with clients and increase their success. To move Amy's sales process along, we began by establishing the Rise Framework for the new employer's business. I'm afraid I cannot share the framework for this company because Amy was our client, and not the company. I can tell you that some of their proprietary technologies supported a compelling Rise Framework that provided Amy with the ability to convey the proposition in 30 seconds, three minutes, 30 minutes, or three hours.

We had to spend extra time practicing with Amy, as she was less comfortable selling and more comfortable connecting—but we made it there. We also became very intentional about planning every single step of the customer journey with a stock of customizable communications that could be delivered at the right time. To her credit, Amy made the commitment to want to grow and evolve and allowed us access to her conversations, processes, and practices.

Breaking through the Schmoozer Mind Trap for Amy involved the following steps:

- It all began with awareness. Amy had never recognized how these Mind Traps worked against her. We worked through the history of specific deals that were lost, making direct connections between Mind Trap and lost sale. Shifting this became a huge motivation.

- We practiced the use of her Rise Framework repeatedly, which was much more conversational than an elevator pitch so it felt natural. This also let Amy out of Feature Listing mode.

- Amy gained confidence presenting her product offering and because she could be more serious about the product, her clients in turn took her more seriously.

- We developed materials to support Amy through the sales journey, and because she was our private client, the company assumed it was her good work that elevated her with her team.

- We focused on a few key features of Salesforce and clarified how she could use her admin to enter and use that information on her behalf. That way she was compliant with management expectations.

- We established a point where company leadership would join in the later stages of getting to the close. This was the part she was least comfortable with and where leadership was most comfortable and rewarded. Everybody was happy!

With the added focus of the Rise Framework, Amy elevated her sales approach and now consistently closes 100 percent more than what she used to do under her own Schmoozer tactics and is making serious money. Now that is progress!

Target Impact

Another important shift was being much more mindful of who Amy spent her time with. In the past, she would keep circling back to the same network of individuals who were fun and connected, but who rarely turned into sales. She did this because she did not know what else to do. We went to a balanced approach. As I shared earlier, great salesmanship will put nearly equal emphasis on three areas: 1) brand; 2) critical features; 3) the salesperson themself. We also became serious about adding prospects to the top of the funnel each month.

Her considerable network had always been willing to help introduce her to other prospects, but they had been wanting her to be more professional before doing so. As Amy shifted, her network shifted with her and we were careful to nurture small early wins into taking the next step in her career. This was so rewarding to witness!

Culture Change

The company was drawn to the Rise Framework Amy was now using and incorporated much of it into their brand presentation. This included not only the language, but also many of the collateral materials we had helped develop for Amy's use. In the past, Amy had actually eroded some culture elements as she had placed a strain on relationships and resources. Now she was emerging as a respected leader, unifying and uplifting the fabric of the company.

The combination of Rise Framework building, supporting materials, training efforts, and people who could fill the gaps in the journey was the winning formula that helped Amy—and the company—to the next level. Perhaps even more importantly, everyone's expectations and strengths worked as a cohesive and powerful machine. Often the combination of growing skills, shifting expectations, and distinctive brand building is what makes it all work.

Comments from Amy

"Selling over the course of my career has been frustrating at many of the companies I have worked at. My former employers have just wanted to use me for my network and because they didn't offer me real support, many times the business fell flat, which hurt my reputation with people who know me. Now I see the role I was playing in driving those perceptions and how I was using the company and how they were using me.

"Once I saw the Mind Trap in myself, and made the commitment to shift it, I elevated my game to be taken seriously and close deals. To be candid, I have always hated the elevator pitch. My friends know me and launching into a spiel like that would just come across as ridiculous. The Rise Framework makes all this natural and conversational and I can fit naturally with where my prospect is coming from in terms of time and interests.

"And lastly, having materials and clarity about how I can work with other people in the company and systems that can help me has been big. Everything used to be unstructured and inconducive to my success. I feel more respected and more powerful as the person I have always wanted to be but did not know how to be."

PART FOUR

TIME TO RISE

Defining the Steps for Your Rise and Illustrating My Own

I truly believe the process of illuminating your Mind Traps and then building your Rise Framework to overcome them will be a process that will provide you with life-changing direction. My goal is to help you Claim the Top of Your Mountain. To do this within the limiting constraint of a book, I have laid out the step-by-step process we follow to build Rise Frameworks and transform client companies.

I have had to do my own illuminating and my own rising to get to where I am today. I have shared my personal struggles and the ups and downs I have had in my own career. It is my hope that my story will give you the hope and motivation to keep moving forward on your own journey.

I would also be remiss if I did not acknowledge the people who helped me rise. We cannot live this life alone, and we definitely cannot succeed without people to strengthen us along the way. I have mentioned throughout these case studies that if this process seems too hard for you to do alone or you don't have people in your own circles to help you, remember you are not alone in this process. Please do not hesitate to reach out to our team. We would be so honored to help you Rise and this can be pretty hard to do for yourself—particularly as a first timer.

CHAPTER EIGHTEEN

START YOUR ASCENT: BUILDING YOUR RISE FRAMEWORK

———————■———————

This book has already given you the foundational information we use to work with clients. This chapter provides the specific steps you need to illuminate your Mind Traps, build your Rise Framework, and start making changes to your company that increase your ability to Claim the Top of Your Mountain. Here they are, in order:

1. Mind Trap Recognition
2. Extreme Empathy Exercise
3. Client/Prospect Interviews
4. Building the Rise Framework
5. Reward and Risk Assessment
6. Reflection and Finalization

This might sound arrogant or maybe even too good to be true, but the work we do with clients has been seriously impactful and even transformative 100 percent of the time. Taking the time to create your Rise Framework will focus you, your teams, and your company to move forward in the same united direction. I am super proud of this process and I am 100 percent confident that it will work for you.

Step 1: Mind Trap Recognition

As this book has outlined, you can't fix a problem you don't know exists. The 10 Mind Traps can seriously erode conversion rates and impact at both a company and individual level. Now that you know *everyone* has Mind Traps, work to recognize yours and have each member of your team reflect on the Mind Traps you collectively need to overcome.

Recognition of these Mind Traps becomes a great catalyst for change. You want to be onto yourself and your tendencies. I also point them out because you need to be aware of yourself, so you don't keep slipping back into your old patterns. The reality is that those Mind Traps that are more personality-based are harder to shed than others because they have become habits. It becomes harder to shake them off, and it takes practice and accountability partners to help us avoid slipping back into our old ways.

Step 2: Extreme Empathy Exercise

The next step is to deeply engage your empathy and look at your business, your offering, and your customers from an unbiased third-person vantage point. This is the beginning of the process of finding the Mountaintop you want to claim. Looking at the following categories will help you define the problem you uniquely solve in the world and move you toward that summit:

- Review existing sales and marketing materials through the eyes of your prospects.

- Describe and size the target market you serve with a very honest and human lens of life with and without your product in it.
- Clarify your competitive strengths/weaknesses with honest self-reflection.

Step 3: Client Interviews

Whenever possible, we like to interview approximately five to 10 current clients or prospects in a safe environment where they can speak freely. This process helps you more clearly define your unique strengths. It also can reveal the unmet needs and white spaces in the market that you can grow into. We like to cover the following items in these client/prospect discussions:

- Background information about them and their company/institution
- Current use of your offering relative to competitive offerings
- What's working well with your offering and what could work better
- Existing unmet needs they experience at each step of the customer journey
- Reaction to concepts or marketing materials for the company's proposition, if applicable
- Advice they would give to the CEO

With the answers to these questions, make a list of your company's assets and gaps as well as any unserved needs in your industry.

Step 4: Building Your Rise Framework

We like to start by comprehensively listing your assets and unique strengths at the level of Proof Points. Don't try and start with your Pillars or Promise. Put your strengths into three buckets.

1. The first bucket will be **Product Benefits,** covering what is distinctive about your process or product.
2. The second bucket can be about the **Emotional Benefits** your offering provides to those you serve.
3. The third bucket can be about the nature of the **Relationship** you foster between yourselves and your customers.

After brainstorming the list, rank them from most to least valued through the eyes of your prospect. This is the draft of your **Proof Points**.

The next step is to develop headings for each of these three categories of Proof Points. What is the gestalt of what these Proof Points would convey? These become your **Pillar Headings**.

The next question is to ladder up what the Pillars would logically sum up to as a conclusion that becomes your **Promise**.

Finally, at the bottom of your Mountain, fill in the operational elements that would be necessary to deliver your Proof Points. These become your **Power Plant**.

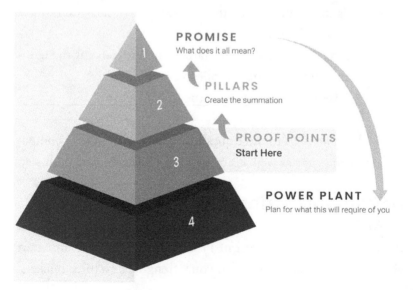

Be open to incorporating unmet market needs that you can reasonably weave into your offering. A great framework has the best of what you are today with an aspirational quality of what you can incrementally provide in the future.

Keep in mind that building your Rise Framework relies on three essential aspects. All your messaging must be:

- **True** of the workplace values of those who labor within the company.
- **Meaningful** in the hearts and minds of your target.
- **Distinctive** with respect to the competition.

In addition, I have described how easy it is to fall into generic language and platitudes that customers increasingly ignore. After you draft your Rise Framework, do a review to make sure that none of the language smacks of generic marketing speak and attempt to deeply visualize how you would feel about your evolved storyline through the eyes of those you seek to serve and adjust as necessary.

Step 5: Risk Assessment

Next you will want to consider potential risk elements being conveyed either by what you are saying or not saying. Filtering your messaging and customer experience for potential risk aspects is key to winning clients or prospective clients. Remember that sellers sell benefits, but buyers buy on risks. This is when third-person thinking is vital—because oftentimes only a single overlooked risk element may be the thing that kills a deal. We are constantly vigilant to these risks because they are as important or more important to impacting conversion rates as benefits being conveyed.

It is incredibly difficult for brands to do all this work internally. It is nearly impossible not to become insulated in our businesses and lose perspective of what it is like to be a prospect.

Find someone to help you see the gaps you cannot see. Remember, it's not the gap itself. We are looking to solve Exponential Risk Escalators that the human mind naturally runs to because we are so wired to avoid risks.

Step 6: Reflection and Finalization

The Rise Framework helps companies focus on their customers and see their assets in order to say what they have always wanted to say about themselves. When you are done with your Rise Framework messaging, the language will feel both familiar and foreign because it is a new way of articulating the company and proposition. It can take a little time to get used to.

One of my favorite ways of testing if you have landed in the best place is to see if the language starts getting used naturally during the first week or two because the team is drawn to it. This is the single greatest validation that it works. Watch for this in your company. Your team should feel like they are expressing the best of themselves and be drawn to start using the messaging because it feels like the right direction. If parts feel forced, then rework those elements to finalize your Rise Framework. Once it is landing, unify your culture, operations, and communications around this structure.

This is the process. These are the solutions. These are ways to take your existing brand and business to become the best version of yourself to break through and serve the world in unprecedented ways. Business and life become a whole lot more beautiful with these revelations actively in play every day of your business. Thank you for reading this book. I hope it has been of service to you. I would love to hear from you.

Illuminate and Rise!

CHAPTER NINETEEN

MY RISE: LEAVING FEAR AND FARMING TO FIND PURPOSE AND HEALING

———————

"To thine own self be true."

-Polonius in *Hamlet*, William Shakespeare

I was not born into branding and business building. In fact, I was born on a farm and was the youngest of four children born to Robert and Elsie Harrison, where I was raised to help build the family dairy farm in upstate New York. Those formative years, I call Doug 1.0, were spent working really hard.

They were particularly important for my development because I learned to see what needed and could be done, and was often directing, from a very young age, daily plans of operations and fixing problems as they emerged on our 500-acre dairy farm. My parents used to tell me I never had a childhood and I never really wanted one. I wanted to be productive. It was an amazing training ground for teaching my brain to see things as they are and what to do about it to create a desired outcome.

I loved and hated farming. I loved the intensity of striving every day to get as much done as possible and seeing what could be accomplished. I loved transforming fields from dirt to crops, taking lifeless ground and making it rich. I loved studying potential genetic matches of bulls and cows to try and produce the ideal offspring that would win awards and produce lots of milk.

I loved how strong I felt seeing what my body could endure, but most of all I loved the camaraderie of working with my older brother. While my two sisters were involved as well and I loved them dearly, my big brother and I were a great team, naturally complemented each other in the work that needed to be done and were just soulmates when it came to work.

What I hated about farming was always being behind. I hated that I was the poor, smelly farm kid growing up in an affluent preppy town. I hated that even among farmers, we were the second tier and watched neighbor farmers win the battle for more land and more scale. At that time, what I hated most of all was that I viewed my dad as a narcissist who cared little about me or my siblings other than what we could produce.

I felt that even though I was pretty much an ideal kid for the farm, I could never gain his approval. I grew up hiding my feelings of pain, hatred, and rage behind a clever class-clown persona. And, like all first-rate martyrs, I turned that hatred and rage inward on myself, furious I could not be more than I was.

Leaving the family farm was a brutal decision for me. When I finally worked up the courage to tell my dad I wanted to leave, he told me he would just sell the whole thing. This, of course, meant my selfish decision to leave the farm would ruin the lives of my parents and siblings, and all of it was my responsibility. I spent a few years trying to convince myself to stay home and do this for my family. For those same few years, I used to pray to die nearly every day just to have some relief from the constant pressure. This was the lowest point of my life.

Luckily, fortunately, divinely, I connected with Kim Adams. She loved me and supported me through high school and those difficult years, and I credit her for helping me survive those years to find my own way and happiness. We have now been married for over 30 years and raised two beautiful children I love more than life itself.

I completed my two-year Ag business degree from an Ag & Tech school and then worked a semester on the farm—following the prescribed path my dad had set for me and my older siblings. But unlike my big brother and sisters, I was miserable. I just couldn't do it. So that spring I started at Cornell University to get my Agricultural Economics degree, which was common practice for Cobleskill grads. Ag Economics at Cornell was the equivalent of a business degree at other schools, but at state school prices. That program was a way of keeping one foot on our farm, which was only 45 minutes from school, and one foot out the door to start a life in business. But when I finally graduated, I didn't go back to the farm and it felt like the ultimate betrayal to my family.

But, in my heart, I was really trying to help. I had always blamed what I perceived as our family dysfunctions on being poor and my young mind thought if I could make us prosperous, all would be right in the world. I carried that into my professional career and hoped I could start a great business, share that money with my family, and all would be well. But I couldn't do it fast enough. Seven years after I decided to leave the farm, the bank told my dad they were no longer going to keep financing the farm.

He died that same year at the unfair age of 63. I think it broke his heart. I was 29.

Over the decades, I have reconsidered and rewritten my childhood story with a good deal of therapy and reflection. I have grown to have tremendous love and appreciation for all of it. I am incredibly grateful for the love of a family that was finding its way, just like any other. My fear of disappointing my dad and feeling at risk in my home environment led to my ability to deeply empathize with others, which is a skill hugely responsible for my success. For the first time in my life, I can honestly look in the mirror and feel love instead of loathing. And that, my friends, is a remarkable gift.

Doug 2.0

I already described at the beginning of the book my career in business. This was the major reinvention of my life. Right after graduating from Cornell, I married Kim and moved to Westport, Connecticut to work with marketing firm Yankelovich, Clancy, Shulman. That was the beginning of my professional career, outside of farming and in the world of market research and consulting. After nine years with them, I was running the strategic research part of the business and had learned a ton about sales, marketing, and product forecasting, having accurately projected the business potential for hundreds of new product offerings and relaunches of existing brands. The problem was that I was no longer learning anything there and was making the company a whole lot more money than I was, so I left and started my own firm with 10 clients who said they would follow me.

We did well and I went from zero to five million dollars overnight and was feeling confident, so I self-funded some technology innovation, which came back to haunt me. I experienced the thrill of victory and agony of defeat like every other entrepreneur

I have ever known. Looking back, I aced my accounting courses at Cornell and part-time MBA program at NYU, but still knew nothing about how to use a financial statement when things were not going well.

This gap became incredibly clear when I took an investment from an outsider who joined the company. He ended up stealing from the company in a very significant way. As terrible as that was, I did learn financial management and how to survive by stretching vendors and negotiating terms. It was a costly but valuable lesson. I also learned the importance of running my business around ratios . . . to operate where each expense line item was managed to not exceed a certain percentage of total revenue. And I have used that method ever since.

We returned to our core business and rebuilt the firm. Dr. James Taylor joined the company and we launched our wealth practice with the first ever quantitative survey of people with ultra-affluence. The top half of one percent. That attracted a partnership with American Express and we became recognized as the top firm explaining the minds, hearts, and spending of affluent and ultra-affluent people as we expanded our coverage to the top 10 percent of the global economy. We had about 50 luxury brand clients when I sold the company with two successful books, *The New Elite* and *Selling to the New Elite.* Many of the foundational techniques I laid out in this book originated with Jim, and I continued to evolve and perfect them.

It was at that point that Deloitte wanted to buy the company and we thought we wanted to sell to them. And then two bad, unforeseen things happened that humbled us again. First, the 2008 financial crisis hit. While we were definitely not the only company to be affected by this, it was rough. Second, we were hacked.

Part of our business was video game testing, that Paul Lundquist did a masterful job running. We assessed video game concepts for all the big publishers and guided and optimized all of their evolution through escalating stages of development. At the time, our company was testing 46 games from companies like Activision, Xbox, EA, Disney, Wizards of the Coast, and others. The hackers posted all of the games on the internet. It was absolutely horrible and had massive ramifications to our business. We lost all of the gaming accounts temporarily, literally millions of dollars in revenue overnight, and while Deloitte still wanted to buy us, it was discounted enough to not inspire me to sell.

We rebuilt again. We fired on all cylinders to make a comeback and won back nearly all our gaming clients. We refined our own Rise Framework, and I connected with another individual who showed me how he used to fight for every point of margin at his company. We used the same tactics and maximized revenue and profitability. At that point, we were approached again, this time by YouGov, a British firm. At first, I was not that interested, but then elected to sell. I did not want to face another downturn in the company's value so we sold it at the optimal time. I was happy to take the chips off the table.

If you too are an entrepreneur, you'll have your own ups-and-downs stories. All entrepreneurs do. The best any of us can hope for is that our successes outweigh our failures. Without question there is an element of luck in there mixed in along with skill. But for me, it has all been worth it. We all worked very hard, but we also took a great amount of pride in taking care of our own, especially when personal tough times arose.

My favorite day of the year was always the company holiday party when all the employees and their significant others came together in a very fun celebration. That was the one night each year when I would pause to reflect on the lives of families we were helping to build. They were happy, they were learning, they were feeding their families, they were supporting their homes, and they were building a life our company was helping to create. I was prouder of that than anything else. This is the strong connection I have with the entrepreneurs and the people I work with now—I just want to share what I've learned and help entrepreneurs avoid as many painful lessons as possible so they can also make the dreams and goals of the families supported by the business a reality.

Finding the path to a solution for a business that is real and works is more gratifying than anything I can possibly imagine. These days I am working increasingly with small to midsize companies because of the magnitude of impact I can have there. The reality is everything I am expressing in this book applies across any business or company. This process will work for you too.

Doug 3.0

So now, I am entering Doug 3.0, which is the manifestation of the best of everything I have learned and all I am able to do to help businesses and people. Most of what I do is focused on evolving businesses to be the best version of themselves. Some people refer to me as a brand whisperer, which is kind of cool, but I also carefully look for opportunities to be of service to the human side of personal growth where it is desired. The world pays attention to how dysfunctions manifest themselves in our personal lives, but the reality is those same dysfunctions play out in professional environments where people are actually spending more of their day. My reality is that I have worked through an awful lot of emotional stuff over the course of my life so when I recognize a need and am invited, I offer help and perspective.

My primary mission in life is to help brands and businesses to become the very best versions of themselves. Everything in this book has been dedicated to that purpose. My experience is that all businesses and people have Mind Traps that work against them. They also have underleveraged assets they could be tapping into more powerfully to better serve unmet market needs. And businesses have the ability to convey the best of all of this to buyers in a more empathetic, more compelling way by focusing on the unique offering they provide to the world. For me, there is nothing more gratifying than helping people manifest this in their lives at the highest degree possible.

Now, as I work with companies, I envision the impact we can have on leadership and all the employees. I imagine their holiday parties and the lives that are growing and progressing because of the work our team is doing. That is the most beautiful gift I can imagine—to feel that I have made a positive change in the lives of others. So, while I wasn't able to help my dad fulfill his dream, it is my enduring hope that now, with a life of experience and knowledge, growth and connection, I can help you fulfill yours.

ACKNOWLEDGMENTS

. . . and Statements of Deep Appreciation

There are several people to whom I especially want to express gratitude for helping me to become the person I am with the skills I have.

Dr. James Taylor was one of the most brilliant brand and marketing minds the world has ever seen. He was a man with an IQ of 186 who consumed and interpreted more content than anyone I have ever known in my life. Many of the techniques shared here were developed, at least in part, by Jim. I owe him a huge thanks and I miss him terribly.

Victoria Sassine has become a close friend and oversaw the Goldman Sachs 10,000 Entrepreneur program. We have been working closely together to further enhance programs that can support lifetime relationships with our entrepreneurial friends through the Rise Club.

Lisa Carter was my early mentor at the beginning of my career from whom I learned volumetric forecasting. Lisa has a brilliant mind and, in many ways, became the unofficial Chief Problem Solver at Yankelovich Partners. It was like working through a whirlwind of business problems in my years there with her. I was very fortunate that she joined me at Harrison Group years later, leading the Coca-Cola relationship.

Scarlett Lewis is the founder of the Choose Love Movement who graciously invited me to be the board chair of this wonderful organization that provides no-cost social and emotional education to millions of kids and thousands of adults who are looking for a more fulfilling way to engage in the world. Scarlett lost her son Jesse in the Sandy Hook school shooting and found the love to turn that tragedy into service. I am grateful for the opportunity to do my part to be supportive in this endeavor.

Melinda Shaha helped me a great deal in getting this book over the finish line and I am very grateful to her. There is a great deal of content swimming around in my brain and having outside perspective and organization that Melinda was able to provide helped so very much. Thank you.

Paul Lundquist was the first to join me at Harrison Group and successfully led the gaming practice of the company for many years. He knows how to serve clients, is a great friend, and is a heck of a drummer!

Nancy Palmer is a dear friend who was clever enough to suggest and build each of the icons associated with each of the Mind Traps. I think she did a great job and I am very grateful!

Dimitri Therios. My man. Thank you for supporting me and my family in our efforts to live our best life. It has been transformative.

Arlyn Lawrence's editing, and her team at Inspira Literary Solutions, provided the final step in getting the book to the level I required. I have appreciated Arlyn's quality, integrity and kindness throughout this entire process.

Morgan James Publishing—Thank you for choosing to publish my book and appreciating the content and meaning you recognized I was hoping to bring to the world.

ABOUT THE AUTHOR

Doug Harrison, as the founder of Harrison Group, has helped guide the branding and business strategies for over 1,000 small-, mid-, and enterprise-size companies. He has been Vendor of the Year at Coca-Cola and a Finalist at Microsoft, and helped shape  the branding, messaging, and targeting for UnderArmour, The Ritz-Carlton, Starbucks, T-Mobile, Amazon, and Mercedes-Benz, in addition to many small-to-mid-sized companies.

Most video games go to market through an evolution process Doug's company created and his firm would serve 50 luxury brands annually in partnership with American Express. He has co-authored two top selling books on selling to wealthy and affluent customers.

Doug's newest book, *The Rise Framework*, is creating awareness of 10 previously unrecognized "Mind Traps" that impair individuals and their businesses from realizing their full meaning and potential in the world. Doug regularly shares the Rise Framework with compelling case studies to reveal what to do about them. He holds a BS in Business and Marketing from Cornell.

Victoria Sassine

Doug recognizes the valuable work of and collaboration with Victoria Sassine, and her signification contribution to this book.

Victoria is the co-founder of *Scale Smarter Partners,* a consulting firm focused on strengthening small businesses. At Babson College, she helped craft and launch the *Goldman Sachs 10,000 Small Business Initiative,* an educational program that created thousands of new USA jobs, and generated millions of dollars in new revenue.

A seasoned *Fortune 500* executive, Sassine has advised thousands of entrepreneurs with a laser focus on owner's wealth creation. She serves as an Audit Chair and Board Director for both public NYSE and private firms. She has an MBA from University of Chicago and is a CPA.

ENDNOTES

1 "Loneliness Is at Epidemic Levels in America." *Cigna News-worthy*. https://www.cigna.com/about-us/newsroom/studies-and-reports/combatting-loneliness/. Accessed 12 September, 2022.

2 "U.S. Population by Sex and Age 2021." Statista Research Dept. https://www.statista.com/statistics/241488/population-of-the-us-by-sex-and-age/. Accessed 12 September, 2022.

3 "Edmund Hillary and Tenzing Norgay Reach Everest Summit." History. https://www.history.com/this-day-in-history/hillary-and-tenzing-reach-everest-summit/. Accessed 12 September, 2022.

4 Young, Emma. "Lifting the Lid on the Unconscious." *New Scientist*, 25 July, 2018. https://www.newscientist.com/article/mg23931880-400-lifting-the-lid-on-the-unconscious/. Accessed 12 September, 2022.

A free ebook edition is available with the purchase of this book.

To claim your free ebook edition:

1. Visit MorganJamesBOGO.com
2. Sign your name CLEARLY in the space
3. Complete the form and submit a photo of the entire copyright page
4. You or your friend can download the ebook to your preferred device

Morgan James
BOGO™

A **FREE** ebook edition is available for you
or a friend with the purchase of this print book.

CLEARLY SIGN YOUR NAME ABOVE

Instructions to claim your free ebook edition:
1. Visit MorganJamesBOGO.com
2. Sign your name CLEARLY in the space above
3. Complete the form and submit a photo
   of this entire page
4. You or your friend can download the ebook
   to your preferred device

Print & Digital Together Forever.

Snap a photo   Free ebook   Read anywhere